CHRIST-CENTERED
GENEROSITY

CHRIST-CENTERED
GENEROSITY

Global Perspectives on the
Biblical Call to a Generous Life

R. Scott Rodin, Editor

The Global Generosity Network

and

Kingdom Life Publishing

Endorsements

Many of us in the Majority World have gratefully experienced the generosity of our sisters and brothers in the West. This book will enrich the global church by showing that stewardship and generosity are not to be confined to a certain culture but are characteristics of an authentic Christian lifestyle. R. Scott Rodin has done a marvelous job by weaving in biblical and theological truth with real-life stories from around the world. I do hope that this book will become required reading for theology students who are preparing to serve God's kingdom.

REVEREND RIAD KASSIS, PHD, International Director, International Council for Evangelical Theological Education, Director of Langham Scholars, Langham Partnership

Our God in love created space for humans and the world to exist as a dependent reality upon Him. As humans we are interdependent upon one another and on God's beautiful creation. God is not a demander, but a giver. We are His guests and recipients of divine provision. The word of God was the chief actor in all that was created (John 1:3). However, when the word became flesh, we crucified Him (John 1:11–14). We were not at all hospitable to the One who is our ultimate Host. Aren't we human beings constantly building walls, shutting people out, slamming our front door in the face of other people and other creatures? We treat creation as an object to dominate. In our consumer-driven culture, things are valued for their usefulness to humanity rather than for what they are as creations of God. This book reminds us that being generous is the very purpose of our creation and redemption in Christ.

REV. DR. RICHARD HOWELL, General Secretary, Evangelical Fellowship of India, General Secretary, Asia Evangelical Alliance

I can highly recommend this book for all people who want to know the heart of God — this is expressed best in generosity. He loved, so He gave!

PETER J. BRISCOE, European Director, Compass — Finances God's Way

The publishing of *Christ-Centered Generosity* is timely, and it is a must-read book for any Christian that desires to grow in stewardship. It offers sound biblical understanding on acquisition and distribution of wealth. The book is relevant to Africa's situation today. It is true that Christianity is growing in Africa; unfortunately, giving to missions is not commensurate to the enormous mission opportunities. *Christ-Centered Generosity* will set the reader free from the tyranny of materialistic tendency that does not satisfy but robs one of the joy of living. Understanding the message of *Christ-Centered Generosity* will liberate and help the reader to look upon the "things" above.

Dr. Duro Ayanrinola, General Secretary, All Africa Baptist Fellowship (AABF)

Just imagine the global and eternal impact if God's people, instead of hoarding His blessings and resources, would release them and invest them for a global mission! This volume provides both biblical truth and testimonial inspiration that help give us a glimpse into what happens when God's people live out biblical generosity.

Dr. Michael Young-Suk Oh, Executive Director/CEO, The Lausanne Movement

A pastor friend from Singapore once told me that during the remarkable growth among Christians there in the 1980s, his church taught new converts four things within four weeks of discipling: how to read the Bible, how to pray, how to share their new faith, and how to give. Generous giving was seen as integral to biblical discipleship, and so it was taught from the very beginning. Generosity is of course a response to grace and an overflow of gratitude. But it is also a matter of obedience (in both Old and New Testaments) and a matter of justice (not charity), as we see in Deuteronomy 15. I commend this book for combining biblical principles with practical examples and for helping us to see that this is not just about "the West funding the rest," but of a mutual and reciprocal duty and joy by which the whole church can be blessed, and the world can come to know the greatest gift of all.

Christopher J. H. Wright, International Director, Langham Partnership, Author of *The Mission of God*

From the first pages of the introduction to the last pages of the Seven-Day Generosity Challenge, this work teaches and illustrates, by principle and example, that generosity is not what we *do* but who we *are*. Filled with stories from all over the world—of much and little, young and old, rich and poor environments—the examples of joyful obedience and the immeasurable blessings that follow serve to encourage and motivate the Christian reader to greater acts of generosity: the manifestation of a transformed life.

Robert C. Doll, Chief Equity Strategist, Nuveen Asset Management, LLC

For one to begin to appreciate the great changes that could impact so many lives—giving them hope and relief in the mess of a world where poverty and ignorance reign—could be possible only through the intentional application of biblical Christ-centered generosity, which is very clearly communicated in this insightful book. Thank you for such a book. I very highly commend this book, which challenges believers to respond to very clear, christo-apostolic admonitions about generosity.

REV. DR. STEVE ASANTE, Immediate Past President, Ghana Baptist Convention

In this book deep biblical theology and down to earth practical application marry to something that could re-shape the face of Christianity. The contributors from all continents prove how a global spiritual concept can and has to be adapted in any given local situation.

THOMAS SCHIRRMACHER, PhD, ThD, DR. PHIL, Chair of the Theological Commission of World Evangelical Alliance, President, International Society for Human Rights

Christ-centered Generosity is a compelling invitation to follow Jesus in being open hearted and open handed. Generosity reflects a foundational dimension of God's nature, giving rise to so many other important expressions of His heart. The book provides biblical insight and practical encouragement, transcending cultural and denominational distinctions, enabling relevance to believers anytime and anywhere."

DAVID E. HAZZARD, Assistant Superintendent for Fellowship Services, The Pentecostal Assemblies of God

The majority of people around the world have fears about losing their jobs, their money, their investment, their possessions. It could be one of the major obstacles for being generous. Only a certain confidence in a Loving God Provider can give us the impulse to start a life with generosity. All the time we need to be challenged and encouraged to understand that the life without fears is a generous life. This book offers a challenge to change your lifestyle, no matter where you live or your social and financial condition. All of us are called to be generous. Take the seven day challenge that this book offers, and I guarantee you that you won't be the same."

DR. FRANK GONZALEZ, Latin America Ministry Expansion Officer, Crown Financial Ministries

Contents

Part VI

Preface

In June 2013 in Bangalore, India, the Global Generosity Network organized a Generosity Summit. Two years later, Indian attendees and presenters have formed the National Generosity Network, which is now organizing a National Generosity Network Leaders Gathering in February 2015. Mr. P. K. D. Lee, an author in this book, started another initiative called the India Generosity Summit and is planning its flagship event for May 2015. Through these efforts, the message of biblical generosity is spreading across the church in India.

This is just one example of a global movement of generosity catching fire in the body of Christ. This book is intended to help feed that fire. The Global Generosity Network has been a leader and catalyst in this movement, and Kingdom Life Publishing produces resources to help God's people be free and joyful stewards of life. We have joined forces to create *Christ-Centered Generosity.*

This project has been blessed to have the participation of thirty-three authors from twenty-two countries. Each has generously contributed their best thinking and shared personal experiences to create this book.

Collectively, our intent and prayer is to provide the worldwide body of Christ with a witness to the transformative power of generosity. We hope these essays and reflections will unite readers with inspiring stories of generosity from people on five continents and from every walk of life.

The book has six parts, the first five of which each open with a theological essay followed by three generosity stories and ending with a personal reflection. The final part concludes the book with challenges set out by leaders from seven international ministries to help readers put what they have learned into practice. This Seven-Day Generosity Challenge is our gift to you, that you may experience the joy and blessing of being a follower of Christ whose heart has been made rich toward God.

May God bless you as you read these stories and take this challenge. And may the movement of global generosity continue in and through you and your witness in your family, church, and community.

SAS CONRADIE, Global Generosity Network

R. SCOTT RODIN, Kingdom Life Publishing

Foreword

After the end of the biennial Lausanne leaders' meeting in Budapest, Hungary, in June 2007, Doug Birdsall asked if Sunita and I were prepared to meet two gentlemen who were having coffee at a sidewalk café nearby. We agreed and crossed the street to meet with Terry Douglass and Paul Schultheis and soon discovered why Doug had asked us to meet with them. As we shared and exchanged our stories (over a few hours and several cups of coffee), we discovered that, as individuals who had established and run successful businesses, we had all faced similar issues and challenges relating to our responsibilities for the finances with which we had been entrusted. We had been stirred to ask similar questions, such as: What does the Bible teach about why we should give? How should we give? Where should we focus and target our giving? Are there needs that remain unfulfilled because of our lack of awareness and strategic thinking? Are we guilty of overfunding certain sectors or, alternatively, are the funds we are giving being used as effectively as possible? Were there others who were facing similar challenges and asking similar questions, and would there be strategic value in calling together like-minded individuals to discuss and pray through these issues in greater depth so we can learn from one another and share ideas and good practices?

The result of the meeting in Budapest was the formation of the Resource Mobilization Working Group (RMWG), which developed into the Global Generosity Network in 2011. The RMWG organized various activities at the Third Lausanne Congress on World Evangelization in Cape Town in October 2010. One of the core contributors to the

Christ-Centered Generosity publication gave a presentation during the RMWG semi-plenary session at the Congress. However, it was during the distribution of Stewardship Study Bibles at Cape Town 2010 and the related South African Mission Congress that we realized that there is a need for a good publication on biblical generosity. Thirty-five hundred Stewardship Study Bibles were distributed, while 1,987 participants from 147 countries completed a generosity questionnaire. Nearly fifteen hundred of these respondents indicated that they wanted further information on generosity resources, 1,345 mentioned that they were willing to encourage generosity and stewardship in their areas of influence, and 980 participants showed interest in becoming part of networks that will increase giving and stewardship.

To meet the need for resources on biblical stewardship, generous living, Kingdom-focused giving, and God-honoring fundraising, we started posting resources on the Lausanne Global Conversation[1] and Global Generosity Network[2] websites. Christian leaders tell us how they download the resources and use it in preaching, teaching, and discipleship. Many leaders distribute the resources further through their networks. In this way we believe that millions of Christians across the world are already inspired to better manage the resources God has given them, share more of what they have with those in need, and give more to causes that advance the kingdom of God.

However, we realized that there is a need for a good, easy-to-read book on biblical generosity that could be used by Christians around the world. A book like *The Purpose Driven Life* by Rick Warren or *The Money Revolution* by Dr. John Preston of the Church of England.[3] After various discussions, we decided to ask Dr. Scott Rodin to edit a book with core contributions from five regions of the world, reflections from Christian leaders from a variety of contexts, stories from around the world, and finally a challenge that can help people start living generously along

---

1. http://conversation.lausanne.org/en/resources/browse/category/Resource+Mobilization

2. www.generositymovement.org/

3. www.themoneyrevolution.net/book.htm

biblical principles. The book also includes questions that people can discuss in small groups and information on resources that can help them further in their Christ-centered generosity journey.

We realize that such a publication is a huge risk because different countries are very different culturally. But I trust that the publication will show that generosity is not about wealthy Christians in the West who give some of their small change to poor people in impoverished countries. Generosity should be the lifestyle of every Christian. Christian generosity is based on biblical principles reflecting God's generosity, especially in the way He showed that by His greatest act of generosity—giving His son to reconcile Himself with those enslaved by sin.

I want to thank Dr. Scott Rodin for his incredible work in making this publication possible. I also want to thank the different contributors to the publication. I am privileged to know some of them personally and hope to meet the others in the future. Most of them are in one way or another linked to the Global Generosity Network. A special thanks goes to Tyndale House Foundation for its generous contribution that made the initial development of the book possible and to Kingdom Life Publishing for taking the risk in publishing the book.

The vision of the Global Generosity Network is a worldwide Christian culture of biblical stewardship, generous living, and Kingdom-focused giving. I pray that *Christ-Centered Generosity* will play a significant role in making this vision a reality. For more information on how we can collaborate to achieve this vision, please contact Dr. Sas Conradie at ggncoord@gmail.com.

RAM GIDOOMAL CBE (United Kingdom), Chair, Global Generosity Network
Chair, Lausanne Movement Board of Directors

Introduction

On one occasion an expert in the law stood up to test Jesus. "Teacher," he asked, "what must I do to inherit eternal life?"

"What is written in the Law?" he replied. "How do you read it?"

He answered, "'Love the Lord your God with all your heart and with all your soul and with all your strength and with all your mind' and 'Love your neighbor as yourself.'"

"You have answered correctly," Jesus replied. "Do this and you will live."

But he wanted to justify himself, so he asked Jesus, "And who is my neighbor?"

In reply Jesus said, "A man was going down from Jerusalem to Jericho when he was attacked by robbers. They stripped him of his clothes, beat him and went away, leaving him half dead. A priest happened to be going down the same road, and when he saw the man, he passed by on the other side. So too a Levite, when he came to the place and saw him, passed by on the other side. But a Samaritan, as he traveled, came where the man was, and when he saw him, he took pity on him. He went to him and bandaged his wounds, pouring on oil and wine. Then he put the man on his own donkey, brought him to an inn, and took care of him. The next day he took out two denarii and gave them to the innkeeper. 'Look after him,' he said, 'and when I return, I will reimburse you for any extra expense you may have.'

"Which of these three do you think was a neighbor to the man who fell into the hands of robbers?"

The expert in the law replied, "The one who had mercy on him."
Jesus told him, "Go and do likewise."

In this profound story of the Good Samaritan, found in Luke 10:25–37, Jesus shares many lessons on generosity. I do wonder if the expert in the law left Jesus and experienced the reality that it is better to give than to receive. You see…

Generosity Changes Everything

Sunday, November 28, 1972. It was a big day. A really big day.

I turned eleven, and my parents gave me the greatest gift ever—a blue Schwinn bike, complete with a sparkly banana seat and high handlebars. Before having this bike, I had to walk to school. The bike wasn't just cool. It was going to be the coolest bike in the rack in front of Ben Franklin Elementary School on Monday…and it was!

Friday, December 3, 1972. It was a bad day. A really bad day.

Probably in my arrogance, I was admiring my new bike more than I should. I put it into the bike rack that morning and failed to remember to put the lock on it. I saw it during recess…I took every opportunity to look at it. When I came out at the end of the school day to get my incredible bike and ride home, it was gone! Stolen! It was a long, long walk home that day.

Friday, December 24, 1972. A day I will never, ever forget.

My extended family on my mom's side had driven in from Dallas and Waco, Texas, to spend Christmas with our family. Among the bunch was my great-uncle Bill (his real name was David; I was named after him). Uncle Bill was one tough man, a farmer and a hunter. Uncle Bill lived by himself in an old house where my great-grandparents had lived in Waco. I always remember thinking how poor he was.

Christmas Eve can be magical for an eleven-year-old boy. You can guess what I hoped for but knew I wouldn't receive—another bike. Sure enough, when Santa showed up, Schwinn did not. I knew it was all my fault I didn't have a bike.

After we opened our presents, Uncle Bill called my dad and me into my parents' bedroom. I remember it like it was yesterday. I thought I was in trouble; it was a condition I often found myself in. Uncle Bill pulled out his old leather wallet, opened it up, and took out a crisp, brand-new $100 bill. I had never seen one in my life. He told me he heard about my bike being stolen and wanted to give me that $100 bill so I could go with my dad to get a new bike.

I just stared at it. I couldn't believe it. Tears come even now, as I see this memory so clearly in my mind's eye.

You see, generosity really does change everything. I never looked at Uncle Bill the same. Here was a man who had given far more than he could afford to help a kid get a bike. I had fallen into the hands of robbers; he had seen my need and had mercy on me.

Generosity is a strong, powerful, and mysterious thing. It changes us when we do it. It changes us when it is done to us. That day forever changed that boy and this man. My uncle's generosity changed my heart, my very soul.

This book chronicles the impact that generosity has on the souls of men and women all over the world. A few of the themes you will experience as you read through these pages are:

Generosity Begins with Christ

Christ gave himself that we might have life, joy, abundance, and freedom. You will read about all these themes throughout these pages. We hope you will sense his love for you as you read this and that you will be drawn in an ever-greater way into the joy that comes from living a generous life.

Generosity Is Universal

Generosity is found everywhere, in France, India, Singapore, the United States, Kenya, the Middle East, China, South Korea, Canada, Nigeria, South Africa, Brazil, the United Kingdom, Burkina Faso, Mexico, the Philippines, Australia, and Guatemala! The viewpoints and perspectives in this book are both varied and unified. The lives are distinct, but the word of God is universal. You will take a trip around the world, yet in some ways, you won't feel like you have left home.

Generosity Is Best Shared with Stories

The hope for this book is to speak to the extraordinary movement of generosity that God is initiating all around the world. Never before has there been such a collection of thoughts on this single topic. You will experience a kaleidoscopic view of the many perspectives of generosity.

Thoughts and questions that will encourage and challenge you include:

- Our offerings are valued as Kingdom treasure in Jesus's eyes.
- He promises to give us more than we need so we may touch the lives of those in need.
- In our battle against the enemy, one of our greatest weapons is generosity.
- Does generosity have the power to unite God's people?
- The biblical call to generosity is linked with a vision for an eternal future.
- Living generously reflects to the world the God we serve.
- Generosity is a reflection of the freedom that comes from being in Christ.
- How important is the ability to receive in order to experience true generosity?
- It is our gratitude toward God that forms the basis of our generosity.

The writings are followed by a Seven-Day Generosity Challenge that will help bring the lessons of this book to life in your life.

Generosity Is Worship

Our hope is that you will sense the intimate worship of our Lord and Savior within these pages. That you will be encouraged to look out for your neighbor. That you will often experience that it truly is better to give than to receive.

DAVID H. WILLS (United States), Cofounder & Chair, Global Generosity Foundation, President, National Christian Foundation (US)

PART I

A Vision for the Generous Life

By R. Scott Rodin (United States)

The Life We Seek

God created us for a life of abundance, selflessness, and joy. When He formed us from the dust of the ground, He breathed His Spirit into ours so that we might live each day in the power of that Spirit, reflecting His image to the world around us. God fashioned us as vessels that would overflow with His Spirit and splash out on everyone. In every area of life, He promises to give us more than we need so that through us He may touch the lives of those in need. The depth of our commitment to Christ is witnessed by the extent to which we openly and joyfully let these blessings flow through us into the lives of everyone we meet. This is the life for which we were created, and as we follow Jesus, it is the life we must seek every day.

This is a book about Christ-centered, joyful generosity. The word "generosity" is surprisingly complex and fraught with a number of dangers that we must address if our generosity is truly to be *Christ-centered*. Let's begin by crafting a definition for this rich and challenging word.

Any definition of "generosity" must first distinguish this term from its more secular counterparts. Chief among them is the term "philanthropy." The word itself means the love of humanity. It defines actions that contribute to the betterment of society and the improvement of the quality of life of others. It is almost always associated with gifts of money or tangible assets. While philanthropic acts are laudable in a non-faith-based context, most definitions of the term do not mention the motivation of the gift; they simply refer to the act of giving on behalf of others.[4]

By contrast, Christ-centered generosity is most clearly distinguished from philanthropy by the fact that the motivation of the gift is as important as the act of giving itself. Our actions as generous stewards are not to be devalued. However, throughout the New Testament, Jesus teaches us that money and motivation, money and trust, and money and worship are often at odds with one another. For Jesus, generosity is an attitude of the heart long before it is a description of an act.

In our definition we will make this distinction between "being generous" and "cultivating a heart that is rich toward God." Where we start in this discussion makes all the difference. So for our definition, we will focus on what happens *in our spirit* that motivates us to live our life with a vision of Christ-centered generosity, and then we will treat *how* a person acts generously as the outflow of such a transformed heart.

Three Faith Commitments

We propose that there are three commitments that we make as followers of Jesus Christ that determine the level of generosity that will flow through our life to others.

It's All His

The best way to demonstrate this first faith commitment is to take a simple glass jar and fill it with dirt. Put your jar of dirt someplace where you can see it often every day. It is a most powerful reminder of a foundational biblical truth. Here is what it symbolizes.

First, it reminds us where we all began. As we said earlier, God created all of humanity by starting with a pile of dirt—plain, simple, ordinary soil. He formed it into the shape of a human and breathed His life into it. Our jar of dirt will remind us of our beginning. If you trace your genealogy back far enough, you will come to a pile of dirt. That is where we all began—all of us.

---

4. See, for example, Robert L. Payton and Michael P. Moody, *Understanding Philanthropy* (Bloomington: Indiana University Press, 2008), 28.

Second, that same jar of dirt will remind us that this is also where we will end. Our bodies will return to the earth, and the worms will have their day. The time will come when our bodies will be reduced, yet again, to a pile of dirt.

When you look at your jar of dirt, let it remind you of where you began and where you will end. And here's the critical point: *in between our beginning as dirt and our end as dirt, it's all God's!* Did you hear that? Everything in our life—our time, our job, our money, our possessions, our relationships, our reputation, our identity, our health, our planet, our very life and breath—everything belongs to Him.

If this is true, then what role do we play in our days on this earth? The only role that makes sense is that of a steward. If everything belongs to God, then we are called and tasked with the joyful opportunity to be caretakers of every aspect of our life. We are not owners of anything. We may take a temporary ownership of a piece of land, a car, or a house, and we are called to be faithful stewards of all such things. But we fool ourselves if we ever believe that we are the ultimate owner. God supplies all of our needs lavishly and abundantly in this life, but all that He gives us are purely gifts from the owner to his trusted steward. They come with the directions to manage them wisely, hold on to them lightly, and give them away generously.

If we are to cultivate the heart of a generous steward, the first faith commitment that must be affirmed is that everything, *everything,* belongs to God and God alone. This is not a statement of resignation but a declaration of absolute freedom.

Joyful Obedience

As stewards of the good things of God, we have only one possible way to live. God created us and empowers us to live a life of joyful obedience. It is a life of obedience because we live at the beck and call of the One who owns all things and has created us to do His will in relationship to them. It is joyful because the owner of all things is also the lover of our souls, the One who takes absolute delight in us and wants nothing more than for us to have life and have it abundantly (John 10:10).

It is a life of obedience because it requires us to deny our tendency to pretend that we are owners and to daily surrender everything to Him. It is joyful because He "is able to do immeasurably more than all we ask or imagine, according to His power that is at work within us" (Ephesians 3:20). It is a life of obedience because it places us in direct opposition to the values and standards of the world around us and requires us to take up our cross and follow Him. It is joyful because following Him is the deepest desire of our heart, and the hope we have in following Him does not disappoint because the love of God "has been poured out within our hearts through the Holy Spirit" (Romans 5:5).

We are stewards, and stewards are free to live the obedient and joyful life created for them by their owner. If God owns everything, then we are free to steward what is God's in a way that brings us fulfillment and joy, and blesses the work of His kingdom in every corner of the earth. What a magnificent calling!

Participation in Generosity

Our third faith commitment flows from the other two. It is an acknowledgment through faith that all of our good work in this world is a participation in the great work that Christ has already done for us. All our generosity is participatory—we are invited into a generous life that reflects our participation in Christ's generous life for all of us. There is great value and importance in our acts of participatory generosity, but if God owns everything, then our generosity is always a reflection of God, who so loved the world that He gave. In one real sense, only God can truly be generous.

Consider the following story. A father decides to give a lavishly generous gift to a local charity. He writes out the check and gives it to his son with the request that his son will carry the check and present it to the head of the charity on behalf of his father. The son does so obediently. Upon receiving the check, the leader at the charity begins praising and thanking the son for his incredible generosity. Our first response should be incredulity that this leader would thank the son when all the son did was deliver the check on behalf of his father. The son was obedient and carried out his work as the father asked, which is a critical part of the story. However, imagine how absurd the story would become if the son accepted the praise and thanks as if the gift had actually come from him. It was the father who was generous, and the role of the son was to participate in his father's generosity by carrying out the work he'd asked him to do. When the praise and thanks came from the head of the charity, it was the son's proper obligation and joy to remind the leader that the gift had come from his father and that all honor and glory was due to him and him alone.

So it is with our acts of generosity. If everything belongs to God, then every act of sharing, giving, and generosity are simply reflections of the heart of our lavishly giving God. When we remember this, we will be sure that all thanks and praise is returned to Him. This does not diminish the role we play as faithful stewards. Indeed, God counts on us for that faithfulness so that His work can be supplied through our faithful acts of selfless giving. Yet in the end, all of our very best work is brought up into the greatest act of giving in human history: God's giving of His only son that we may have life and have it abundantly.

Definition

We have attempted to differentiate generosity from the worldly notion of philanthropy, and we have proposed the three faith commitments that are required of us if we are to develop hearts that are rich toward God. We are now ready to offer a definition of Christ-centered generosity:

> Christ-centered generosity is the disposition of a heart that is rich toward God and is a defining characteristic of the life of an obedient and joyful steward.

Freedom From and Freedom For

At the heart of this definition is a twofold freedom. Christ-centered generosity is both a freedom *from* and a freedom *for*. Let's begin with "freedom from." The *Collins English Dictionary* defines "generosity" as follows:

1. willingness and liberality in giving away one's money, time, etc.; magnanimity
2. freedom from pettiness in character and mind
3. a generous act[5]

I love the idea that generosity is a "freedom from pettiness in character and mind." It is a version of a powerful biblical principle of death preceding life. The Christian life is an ongoing process of dying to our sinful old nature and rising to the new life in Christ; sanctification follows repentance, Easter follows Good Friday, and victory begins with surrender.

And so it is with generosity. We must be set free from old, deadly attitudes and habits in order for God's Spirit to cultivate in us a heart that is rich toward Him. Until that happens, our heart will continually seek after those things that will best serve us. The result of this self-serving tendency is bondage. We become enslaved to the things we seek to own and control. The more we desire to possess all things, the deeper we realize that we are the ones in bondage. If we are honest with ourselves, we will be able to trace our stress, fear, anxiety, and despair directly back to those things over which we pretend to play the owner and desire to have control.

In one sense it is impossible for us as owners to be generous. That may sound like a shocking statement, so let me say it in a different way. Only a steward who has been set free can act obediently on behalf of the owner in the generous distribution of what he does not own. Once we yield to the temptation to play the owner, our ability to act obediently and joyfully on behalf of the true owner is lost. That is the reason we must be set free from the chains that bind us in our penchant for ownership.

If you are struggling today with those chains of bondage that come from this ownership mindset, and if you are experiencing the anxiety, fear, stress, and despair that result from this bondage, then these words are for you:

---

5. *Collins English Dictionary* (New York: HarperCollins, 2012).

Then you will know the truth, and the truth will set you free.... So if the Son sets you free, you will be free indeed. (John 8:32 and 36)

Now the Lord is the Spirit, and where the Spirit of the Lord is, there is freedom. (2 Corinthians 3:17)

It is for freedom that Christ has set us free. Stand firm, then, and do not let yourselves be burdened again by a yoke of slavery. (Galatians 5:1)

Claim these rich promises from God's Word as your own. Christ came to set you free from all that would burden you down and enslave you to the life of an owner. Let these words break those chains today—and for the rest of your life. Claim the promise, "If the Son sets you free, you will be free indeed"!

With this newfound freedom, we can look ahead to the life God has for us. We have been *freed for* a life of joyfulness, purpose, and peace. When all of life is viewed from the perspective of a steward, everything changes. Our thirst for intimacy with God will be unbounded. Our identity in Christ will allow us to live in this world free from the need to protect our reputation, hunger after applause, scramble after our own self-advancement, or place ourselves in a position above our neighbors. Humble service, sacrificial love, and selfless generosity flow from the heart that has been set free. From the vantage point of a faithful steward, we will see our neighbors differently. We will gladly care for their needs and love them because we have first loved God with all our heart, soul, strength, and mind, and we have loved ourselves as image bearers of God. From this vantage point, we will also see this world in a different light. We will care deeply for this beautiful creation that God made precisely for us. We will take seriously our first and highest calling to tend the garden, care for the environment, and be guardians and protectors of all that God has created. We will steward our time, invest our talents, and be free and generous with our wealth.

This is freedom in action. When our spirit has been unchained from the shackles of ownership and our heart set free to become rich toward God, our life will be a continuous outflow of generosity. This is the only path to the generous life. It doesn't come by trying harder, feeling shame for our lack of generosity, "giving until it hurts," or executing better financial planning. We will only know true generosity in our life when we have experienced the absolute freedom that only comes through Christ, resulting in the heart of an obedient and joyful steward.

Chained Again

After this rich discussion of our freedom in Christ, it may seem odd to return again to these old chains that lay scattered on the floor around our feet. Paul admonishes us not to become burdened again by these old chains. Yet at the same time, we have an enemy whose sole desire is that we reach down, pull them up over our shoulders again, and lock them in place. The enemy uses lies and deceptions to trick us into placing these old chains back on our shoulders. It is important in this opening chapter to identify three lies that are the most heinous—and effective.

Pride—My Generosity

You will not certainly die…your eyes will be opened.

In Genesis chapter 3, the serpent offers Eve the opportunity to have her eyes opened. He promises that she will see things only God should rightly see, and in seeing she will have the power to grab control for herself and decide on her own terms what is right and what is wrong. Since that original sin, we all struggle with the desire to let our pride rule our life. For followers of Jesus Christ, the same enemy presents it to us as a subtle shift in perspective that seems harmless but starts us down a path to destruction. This is especially true in this area of generosity. It begins by creating in our heart a willingness to consider ourselves as ultimate owners. From there our pride will lead us to see giving as a way to further our own needs and desires. Giving can easily become manipulative—used to bring about recognition, self-satisfaction, and accolades—all under the guise of Christ-centered generosity. We must check ourselves carefully and frequently for this deceptive attitude in our acts of generosity. Even the most magnanimous gift can be tarnished by a spirit of ownership that engenders a sense of great pride in "my generosity, my largess, my great heart," etc.

The cure for this temptation goes back to our simple jar of dirt and remembering that it's all His. Cultivating the heart of a steward requires us to wage battle against all those prideful thoughts and desires that flow from the lips of the enemy. Jesus put it perfectly when challenging the Pharisees in their own prideful giving:

> So when you give to the needy, do not announce it with trumpets, as the hypocrites do in the synagogues and on the streets, to be honored by others. Truly I tell you, they have received their reward in full. But when you give to the needy, do not let your left hand know what your right hand is doing, so that your giving may be in secret. Then your Father, who sees what is done in secret, will reward you. (Matthew 6:2–4)

There may be no better litmus test for the disposition of our heart regarding generosity than in how we would answer this question: would we receive great joy from giving a generous, sacrificial gift anonymously, asking only that God get the glory? We must strive for this attitude in all of our giving and be on guard for any vestiges of pride that may creep up and steal from us the joy of the generous steward.

Power—Generosity as Currency

You will be like God.

Power is pride's companion in deception. We thirst for power in order to gain control of our life. Given the chance, we like to play the lord over the variables in our world. Returning to Genesis chapter 3, the enemy's final offer to Eve is that she could "be like God." The same temptation confronts us every day, in every decision we make that demonstrates who is ultimately Lord of every area of our life. My friend and coauthor P. K. D. Lee says that every decision you make in life is ultimately a decision between serving God or serving money.

Money, possessions, and power are all major players in this battle for lordship. In most Western societies, we are told that power and wealth bring happiness and satisfaction. The business world lauds the powerful and consumes the weak. Our cultural values push us toward working harder, making more money, spending more on ourselves, building our own kingdoms, and shoring up our own power base so that we may be lords of our own lives. Unfortunately, this attitude shows up all too often within the Church of Jesus Christ. We see it with pastors who pretend they are the owners of their church and congregation, and issues of power and control are almost always their downfall. We see Christian business-men and -women separate their work life from their walk with Christ, yielding to secular standards and ethics on the job that too often lead to their ruin. And in our Christian organizations and ministries, issues of money, control, and possessions seem to dominate board meetings and organizational strategies, all in an attempt to gain the greatest level of power and control over our present work and our future ambitions.

At an individual level, when power controls us, generosity becomes a currency we use to keep what power we have and to buy more. We can use our giving to buy favors, open doors, influence opinions, improve business, and purchase reputations. This may sound harsh, yet through the deception of the enemy, it is actually incredibly subtle. Many followers of Christ who have great wealth find it nearly impossible to give it away freely without yielding to some form of this temptation. Even for most of us who have only modest means, the temptation lurks.

The good news is that victory is ours, *and it comes through our absolute surrender*. Surrender makes our thirst for power impotent. The work of the Holy Spirit is to shape in us the heart of a steward to such an extent that generosity becomes a disposition of our spirit, not just an act. We return to joyful obedience as our daily experience on the journey of the faithful steward. Following Jesus Christ is a daily process of surrender, the losing of our life that we may find "the life that is truly life" (1 Timothy 6:19).

In response to the first temptation, we were challenged to do our giving in secret. In response to the second one, we were challenged to make sure all our giving has no strings attached. There is no quid pro quo, no expectation of anything we may gain back from our gift. The generous life is filled with secret giving that desires nothing in return. That is a generosity that reflects the heart of our God and ensures that He always gets the glory.

Praise—Generosity and Recognition

The third temptation is closely aligned with the first two, but it has its own uniquely perverted twist. To understand this temptation, we must return to the issue of identity. As followers of Jesus Christ, we affirm that our ultimate identity is found in Christ and Christ alone. That is, we are content with the affirmation from the lips of our Savior. We seek no other applause than that from nail-scarred hands. Affirmation from others is an important part of living in community, but when it becomes the dominant source of our self-identity, we have stepped off the path.

Think of people who are standing squarely in the center of a road, looking straight down the middle, focused only on Jesus Christ. As long as they keep their focus, they will remain on the road to which God has called them. As soon as they are distracted, looking either to the left or to the right, they will begin to wander into all kinds of dangers.

It is very much like the story of Peter walking on water in Matthew 14:28–30. As long as he kept his eyes on Jesus, he did the miraculous and the water held him. As soon as his eyes were diverted and he saw the wind and the waves around him, he began to sink. So it is with us. As long as our identity is found completely in Jesus Christ, we can live in this world free from the need to constantly prop up our reputation, earn the applause of our peers, or stand in the limelight of recognition from a worldly perspective. We are secure in our identity as a child of the King. As we've said before, this is real freedom.

It is also hated by the enemy. Every day we are faced with the temptation to shift our identity from who we are in Christ to our career or the roles we play in our family, church, or community. We are tempted to allow our self-worth to be influenced by what people think of us and what is expected of us. If we give in to this temptation, we will shift our identity to something other than Christ and lose our singular focus on him. We will begin to sink. One of the indicators that we are sinking is when we thirst after worldly affirmation to prop up our misdirected identity. Think about it for a minute: What are the sources that shape your self-image and self-identity? Whom have you given permission to speak into your life at such a level that a critical word from them can shake your self-image to the core? How closely do you tie your identity to your job, your title, your degree, your accomplishments, or your position? These are all warning signs that we are sinking.

Once again, money, power, possessions, and pride all play a role in this drama. In particular, our acts of generosity become tainted by the desire to use them to gain the affirmation we need to support our misplaced identity. Ironically, this is a particular temptation for those who are most generous. Many wealthy Christians have worked hard to develop a reputation for being generous. And that is exactly the problem. When their reputation for generosity becomes the driving force in their giving, they cease being generous in a Christ-centered way and instead use their giving as a way to further that reputation. That is how subtle and devious the enemy can be. He can quickly turn a lifetime of generosity into a badge of pride, a source of power, and an instrument of praise, all of which tarnish the gift and eat away at the soul of the giver.

The cure is to find our identity and our affirmation in Christ alone. Here again we must remember that Christ-centered generosity is always participatory. We are only generous because we have the opportunity to reflect and participate in the astonishing, lavish generosity of God, who so loved the world that He gave. When we fully embrace that spirit, all desire to use generosity to gain the praise of others fades away.

Our prayer is that in recognizing these three temptations—pride, power, and praise—we might surrender ourselves to Christ so that the Holy Spirit will work in us a heart that is rich toward God. Through such a heart will flow a lifetime of joyful generosity, to the glory of God.

The Seven Victories of the Generous Spirit

A few years ago, a friend introduced me to a revolutionary idea. In our battle against the enemy, one of our greatest weapons is generosity. You may never have considered generosity as a weapon against the enemy. Neither had I. So consider with me seven victories that we win every time we perform an act of giving that flows from a generous, Christ-centered spirit.

In the Battle for My Love between God and Money, I Choose God

In Matthew 6:24, Jesus makes it very clear that each of us will make a choice as to whom we will serve as the Lord of our life. He gives us only two choices: Him or money. Even though we may have read that verse a number of times, its sharpness and unequivocal tenor is shocking. We will either hate Jesus and love money, or we will be devoted to Jesus and despise money. There is no room for a middle ground. This is the first reason why generosity is such a powerful weapon against the enemy. When we have been set free to give generously as God directs us, we rob money of its power to dominate and control us. Every generous act made in the right spirit is a dagger in the heart of this rival god. It is our way to say to the world, "In this great battle for my love between God and money, I choose God."

I Trust God to Be My Provider

Generosity and trust are close allies in this battle. We give generously in part because we trust that God will meet all of our needs according to His glorious riches in Christ Jesus (Philippians 4:19). If we do not believe that God will meet our needs, we can never be the generous and joyful giver He created us to be. Generosity is an act of trust. When we have been set free to listen for God's direction and then respond, no matter how outrageously generous He may ask us to be, we are victors in this great battle. The great missionary to India William Carey wrote, "I was once young and now I am old, but not once have I been witness to God's failure to supply my need when first I had given for the furtherance of His work. He has never failed in His promise, so I cannot fail in my service to Him."

Trust God to be your absolute provider in all things, and watch what amazing generosity will result.

It's All His—I Will Not Pretend I'm the Ultimate Owner

We've already seen the power of this simple little phrase, "It's all His." Here we can see how it becomes a primary weapon in the battle against the enemy. It's why I encouraged you to fill your jar with dirt and put it in a place where you can see it every day. Search your heart for signs of fear, anxiety, stress, or dread, and see if you can trace them back to something that you're holding on to, something you have not surrendered fully to Jesus Christ. The enemy is using that exact thing to keep you in bondage. Your greatest weapon is the freedom that comes through a generous heart. Christ has set you free—embrace the journey of the faithful steward and claim your victory.

I've Been Set Free to Give with Joy

There are a great number of Christians who give regularly, even many who give sacrificially, but do so with little joy. Some have been trained to believe that it is their duty and obligation to give. Others give out of a misconception of the Old Testament concept of the tithe and give mostly out of guilt as a result. Some give out of a sense of gratitude, which can be the other side of the coin from guilt: "God has given you so much, shouldn't you be grateful and give something back?"

There are a lot of motivations in the church for people to give, but Jesus specifically lifted up the joy of Christ-centered generosity. Imagine if taking the offering was a highly anticipated, joyful, and meaningful moment in every worship service. That would require the transformation of people's hearts and the cultivation of Christ-centered generosity. When that happens, when we give with absolute joy, we render the enemy impotent in so many ways regarding money, pride, power, and praise. Pray for that spirit that you may be filled with the joy of the Lord in every expression of obedient generosity.

I Want to Worship God with All I Have—No Withholding

There is a powerful and disturbing lesson that comes from the story of Ananias and Sapphira from Acts 5. The entire church in Jerusalem is experiencing an amazing overflow of generosity. Everyone is selling land and possessions and bringing all they have to put at the feet of the apostles. They do it with joy, understanding that God is their provider, that they have been set free, and that this money is going to be used to bless others and further the kingdom of God. Their giving is a supreme act of worship.

In the midst of this outpouring of generosity, Ananias and Sapphira decide to withhold for themselves part of what they received from the sale of some land. While this may not seem unreasonable at first read, the problem is with the disposition of their hearts. So many of the temptations we've talked about can be found in this story. Their sin is twofold. First, they give in to their sense of ownership and withhold from God what is rightly His, reducing their worship to a financial transaction. Second, they lie about it.

The power of misplaced ownership is such that it multiplies sin, as we see in Acts 5 as well as Genesis 3. If we believe everything belongs to God, then giving is a sacred act. We cannot separate our giving from our intimate life of worship to the Father in the name of the Son by the power of the Holy Spirit. God wants all of us—heart, soul, mind, and pocketbook. It's all His, and He desires that we lay it all before His feet with great joy, anticipating what He will do with it for our good and the advancement of His kingdom. Are you giving joyfully and freely, holding nothing back but responding obediently as God leads you? If so, you've won a great victory in this battle.

Money Has No Hold on Me!

We have acknowledged the power that Jesus ascribes to money. There is no greater way to rob money of this power than to simply give it away. The world around us is telling us that money is the solution to our problems. With more money we can live in our dream house, travel the world, be admired by our friends, control our circumstances, satisfy all our pleasures and desires, and be happy. Of course, it's all a lie, a grand deception. We've seen how the love of money brings nothing but bondage, fear, anxiety, stress, and despair. Our acts of generosity, our free and joyful giving, are a public declaration that we renounce and reject this whole distorted notion about money in our world. We say directly to the enemy, "Money has no hold on me. The Lord provides it, and the Lord guides me in giving it away lavishly and generously. The Lord will take care of my every need, and therefore money has no place in my heart." That is real freedom. That is true victory!

I Worship a God of Abundance, and I Can Never Out-Give Him

Finally, we have the opportunity through our generosity to affirm this wonderful truth that we worship a God of absolute abundance. It is so easy to slide into a scarcity mentality, always focused on what we don't have. We look at the affluence of others with envy and become reticent when friends and peers advance ahead of us. These are signs of a scarcity outlook. In such a mindset, we will never have enough, and therein lies the true deception. When we can be discontent in the midst of all that God has provided for us, we have allowed a spirit of scarcity to take over. This too is a grand lie.

We worship a God of abundance who wants only to provide for us if we will yield our life to Him. By our acts of generosity, we acknowledge God's unfailing abundance. And with it comes the second truth: we can never out-give God. He challenges Malachi, "Test me in this...and see if I will not throw open the floodgates of heaven" (Malachi 3:10). Throughout human history everything we know about God as revealed to us through Scripture and in the life of Jesus Christ tells us that at His very heart He is a giver—an abundant, gracious, lavishly providing, sovereign God. If we believe that, we can live in this world with the freedom to reflect that image in all our acts of generosity. And when we do so, we will know daily victory in this ongoing battle.

Conclusion—A Vision for the Generous Life

The loving God who created you has an amazing vision for your life, and it includes a heart of a faithful steward that is opened up to the world through Christ-centered generosity. We pray that you will embrace that life today. It begins with a simple but profound affirmation: "It's all His." To God be the glory!

Questions for Individual Reflection and Discussion in Small Groups

- What kind of life do you want for yourself?
- Do you recognize the chains that keep you in bondage, that rob you of the life God created you to live, that stress you out and wear you down?
- Are you listening to the lies of the enemy regarding money, possessions, power, pride, and praise?
- Most importantly, do you want to be free?

The Church in Yunnan Province

BY GE JUN (CHINA)

A small church of twenty-plus members in Yunnan province collected ¥246.50 RMB (about $36 USD) during a recent Sunday offering as their relief fund for one of our national partners who has a ministry team in the recent earthquake epicenter in Yushu, Qinghai province. While this may not sound like much, let me tell you more about this faithful little church.

This small church is located in a mountainous area, which itself is in great poverty and in dire need of help. The only crop that grows locally is potatoes. Most families live off two meals of potatoes each day. The average annual income per household is ¥200 RMB, less than $30 USD. This means that this small church of twenty or so members has offered up *more than a whole year of one household income* in this one Sunday service alone to help people in need thousands of miles away, people whom they have never met.

This is a church filled with joyful givers despite their own poverty. They are living examples of 2 Corinthians 8:1–5, where their "extreme poverty welled up in rich generosity"! This is a church whose members give what they have as the widow's mite, each person coming forward with small bills of ½ RMB and 1 RMB (7 cents and 14 cents USD). But their offering is valued as the Kingdom treasure in Jesus's eyes, which God will take and multiply a hundredfold. God certainly honors such kinds of faith in action. We are praying that China becomes more missional and giving, just like this little Yunnan church. May God bless you with a giving heart as well!

Generosity Blesses and Unites in San Marcos

BY LUIS CHAVEZ (MEXICO) AND NYDIA GARCÍA-SCHMIDT
(MEXICO AND UNITED STATES)

D oes generosity have the power to unite God's people? We have seen it happen. In San Marcos, Mexico, the churches faced a problem. James Luna, a Ngigua-language translator, put it this way: "There had been a lot of jealousy and criticism between the pastors of the churches in San Marcos. We tried many times to hold meetings together but it was difficult..."

So when the decision was made by the Ngigua-language translators in Acapulco in 2010 to accept hosting the next National Union of Indigenous Civil Translators Association (UNTI) meeting, there was question as to how the churches would respond. To everyone's joy, the Evangelical Church of the Brethren, who meet in the name of the Lord Jesus, and the Christian Family Center churches were very willing and honored to receive the UNTI group. Both churches agreed that they would host and feed the 120 event participants together, including indigenous translators from all over Mexico and special guests coming from Brazil, Costa Rica, Panama, the United States, and Australia.

Preparations for the event were made for eighteen months, and as the date approached, the hosts were so organized that no logistical detail was overlooked. Four teams were formed: one for cooking, one for washing dishes, another team for cleaning, and a team for serving food.

Each head of household, thirty in all, contributed the equivalent of $85 USD for food. More than eighty church members showed up to volunteer in one of these areas. Besides financial support, people contributed vegetables, fruit, live chickens, etc. A total of 31,000 pesos was raised, equivalent to $2,550 USD.

The average Ngigua family earns 3,600 pesos a month, about $288 USD. For them, the $85 they contributed was equivalent to giving 29.5 percent of their monthly income. Others made personal offerings of $500 to $1,000 depending on family income.

The generous spirit spread to the children, who went with their parents to their fields to gather flowers and vegetables. We saw families arriving with baskets of plants and vegetables to give as offerings for feeding all those attending the meeting. Additionally, everyone worked on food preparation in one way or another—women cooking and making tortillas, men and children carrying baskets of everything needed for preparation, others working to see that the venue was clean and ready for the meetings.

After the meeting there were words of appreciation from one church to the other. There were moments of reconciliation and words of forgiveness. Since then, the churches in San Marcos meet and enjoy fellowship and friendship like never before.

This testimony was shared to recognize the work and effort that the Ngigua brethren made to make us feel at home, and they have given us an example worthy of imitating. When we are generous and open our hearts to others, we cannot remain divided. Generosity brings unity and healing, and unity glorifies God. These churches gave us an example that is based on love for God and one's neighbor. Thanks again, brethren, you are an example worthy of imitation. *Ndo Dio tsjengijna ko sinthanchaon* (May God bless and encourage you even more).

A Chain of Generosity in an Indian School

BY CHITRA V. (INDIA)

One day as I was praying at my home in Bangalore, I had the sudden urge to go visit my old hostel friend named Ganga, whom I had not seen for a long time. In the middle of the prayer, I got up and walked over to her house. She greeted me with her ever-graceful smile, with much cheerfulness, and also offered me water to drink, as per Indian custom. As I was talking to her, I noticed her need, which was everywhere around her—broken floor, broken main door covered by curtains, unpainted house, cracked walls appearing as though they were about to fall, and completely blackened asbestos sheet serving as a roof.

Her children surrounded me with love and hugs. They too were delighted to see their mom's old friend visiting them. She had four daughters and one son. Anjali, the oldest, was in tenth grade, Abhishek in eighth grade, and Ashwini in sixth grade. Anusha was three years old, and Abigail was a year and a half old. As we were talking, Ganga revealed that her husband had married another woman and had two children with her and that he rarely visited this family. He had not provided any financial help. Ganga was working as a caretaker in a nearby children's play home, where she made a meager wage.

I soon realized the children were not in school. Ganga asked me to come talk to their schoolteachers. So the next day, I met their teachers along with Ganga. They told me that the children were very bright students and had the capability to excel with high ranks. However, they had a lot of fees to clear and needed to submit a transfer certificate from their previous school. Moreover, the admissions period was already over, making it impossible to take them in the class.

Abhishek needed be admitted to high school, but without his family paying the dues, the school was not willing to take him. I pleaded with the teachers to give us a week's time in hopes of trying to fix everything. They consented to one week.

I promised Ganga that I would try to somehow collect 500 rupees for the transfer certificate. I asked the Lord in prayer, "Lord, I don't know what will happen to these children's education. While all the others in their neighborhood have access to education, only these three children are at home." This kept troubling me.

The next day I was standing outside my house when a boy approached seeking guidance to open an account. In our conversation I shared Ganga's story, and he immediately stretched a 500-rupee note. I went immediately to Ganga's home with the money for Abhishek, but when I got there, I saw that Ganga was trying to cook some food late at night. Anusha, the three-year-old, was not able to bear the hunger. She was constantly telling her mother to give her food and was requesting of her mother, "Please don't cook late from tomorrow onwards." They barely had enough food for one meal and no means to cook the food. I was so moved by the image of Anusha trying to bear the hunger. I gave Ganga the 500 rupees that I had collected so she could buy food for the children, and I told her that I would make some other arrangement for Abhishek.

The next day I met the bakery shop owner and asked for help for this family, and he gave me 500 rupees. Another person donated three school bags, lunch bags, tiffin boxes, water cans, etc. I shared this need with my aunt Gracy, a prayer warrior and a compassionate person. Gracy promised to pray, and without any hesitation, she handed me 1,500 rupees. I shared this story with a friend of mine, who in turn shared it with his father, who responded by buying books for two of the children. He asked two of his friends, and they paid the school fees for the other two children. By the end of the day, we had paid all the current school fees, the children had gotten their books, and by God's grace, they were able to catch up with their lessons that they had missed.

There was one last generosity miracle. When Abhishek went to be admitted in the new school, the staff told us there was no more admission—everything was closed. Miserable and hopeless, Ganga stood near the principal office's gate. To her surprise, one of our friends, Madhumala, happened to pass by and greet Ganga. Ganga shared her story, only to find out that Madhumala worked for the principal. He went in to persuade the principal to give admission, and the principal agreed if the fee of 4,500 rupees was paid the next day.

Ganga called me up to share this and also the need of 4,500 rupees. I just told her to trust the Lord, and He will do great things. That night as I came out of the house, I saw a girl named Ashwini, with whom I seldom talk. I asked how she was doing in her family life and, wanting to encourage her to trust God, I shared Ganga's story and need. She was anxious to help, wondering why I had not come to her sooner. The next morning she brought 4,500 rupees.

Now by God's grace, three children are studying, and the other two children are going to a government play home. The teachers testified that this is the first year that the children's fees have been paid in full, they have books, and all documents are filed. Praise the Lord.

I share this in detail because there were many different people who participated in this generosity—a chain of both Hindus and Christians in this journey. Through this, God taught me just to be available for Him. If He is sending me anywhere, He will take care of all the details. I only need to go where He sends me. Thank you, God, for teaching me this way.

The Exciting Path

By Suparno Adijanto (Indonesia)

My walk in generosity started when I became a Christian at the age of seventeen. I realized that I have a loving and generous God who does not hold back a single bit but instead died for me. He gave me salvation though grace alone. His love compels me to give my all to Him.

At that time, I learned life is not a dot but an eternal line. Not seventy to eighty odd years here on earth, but eternity. At the end of my life, God will call me to account for that which He entrusted to me. 2 Corinthians 4:18 became my life verse. It encourages us to focus on what is unseen, since what is seen is temporary but what is unseen is eternal. I understand that certain things, such as the souls of men and obedience to God, will last for eternity. On the other hand, worldly things like money, materials, and fame are temporal. This realization leads me to constantly examine my life and ask my Lord, "What would you have me do, Lord?"

Upon graduating, I worked in the family business. As I had a low starting salary, I decided to give more of my time and talents to God's work. Over the years, my salary increased, and I was able to increase my giving while maintaining a faithful application of my time and talents. However, I was also challenged by the Lord to examine what I held in my hands, just as He asked of Moses. I started to strategize and use the businesses and resources entrusted to me, such as the preschools, primary and secondary schools, and the companies' corporate social responsibilities programs to do His will. We began to give out scholarships, to fund disaster relief, and to do community capacity-building programs.

Eight years ago, when I was asking the same question, "What would you have me do, Lord?" the Lord challenged me to teach and mentor more young people in the area of stewardship. At that time, I was the Indonesian representative of Crown Financial Ministries. We started going around the country teaching people how to manage money God's way. We also worked with Rep Ministries to repurpose Indonesian companies to serve God. This year, we started Kingdom Entrepreneurship Academy to equip entrepreneurs to honor the Lord in the business He has entrusted to them. I started to write and speak in the area of stewardship so as to influence more people.

Two years ago, while watching the movie *Schindler's List* for the second time, I was moved by the ending scene. Oskar Schindler, despite having saved hundreds of Jewish lives during the Nazis' occupation, regrets not doing enough. He cries out, "I could have done more. I could have done more." I started asking, "What else can I do, Lord?" At that time, I was reading Timothy Keller's *Generous Justice*. He speaks on the need for social justice, especially in countries where the poor are being oppressed. Yes, teaching a person to fish is better than giving a person a fish. However, if due to some injustice there are no more fish in the lake, social justice may be necessary. Christians must be the proponents of such changes in their society. That began my journey in the transformation path.

Generosity is an exciting path to walk. It is not just about giving money. It involves our time, our talents, and our all. It involves helping to multiply more Christ-like stewards. It includes impacting our societies. We must not stand still.

Will you open your heart and ask God today, "What else do you want me to do, Lord?" And when He speaks, will you obey with joy?

We must not come up short. When I meet my Lord Jesus, I want to hear him say, "Well done, Suparno, my good and faithful servant; enter into the joy of your master."

PART II

Christ-Centered Generosity
and Western European Christians

By Daniel Hillion (France)

People living in Europe show a great variety of cultures. Shifts of populations have resulted in a growing multicultural and multifaith continent. Many evangelical Christians in Europe have non-European roots, and although they represent a small minority, one should be sensitive to the great diversity of their movement. Every attempt to find general characteristics is liable to the charge of caricature.

Yet there is a Western dominant model that more or less influences—or at least puts pressure on—everyone, including Christians. Theologian Henri Blocher speaks of a "covetous society" with advertising as a major feature to characterize the consumerism that is typical of Western postmodern mentality.[6] In the current context, generosity is certainly appreciated as a much-praised value, but it is certainly not sacrificial or Christ-centered.

One should also point to some present overall circumstances. Think of privileged living conditions when compared with those of people in the South[7] (for example, in terms of access to safe drinking water, food, health care, education, social welfare, etc.), but also of economic crisis, significant unemployment rates, fear about the future, and lack of hope.

There can be many different ways to look at the generosity of European Christians in this context. One can try to find statistics indicating what

---

6. See Henri Blocher, "L'avenir du protestantisme évangélique en france à l'aube du IIIe millénaire," *La Revue Réformée* 208 (2000): 5.

7. By "South" I mean roughly economically poor countries, knowing that the North/South divide is not easy to define very precisely. Some would rather speak of "developing countries" or "majority world."

proportion of their income they give to churches, missions, parachurch agencies, etc.[8] Then you could look for the opportunity to compare these statistics to what Christians in other countries give, to what non-Christians in the same countries give to charitable causes, to what the same people gave before they became Christians, or to a normative standard such as tithing, etc. All of these (and other) considerations are relevant and interesting, providing you can obtain reliable information. It would probably give us both signs of encouragement and causes for disappointment.

The Bountiful Eye

It is also possible to look at the generosity of European Christians in the light of what God requires of us or the vision for the generous life sketched in Part I of this book in its full breadth. Then most of us would have to recognize that we still have a long way to go on this journey of the faithful steward and that it hits hard at some features of European culture.

But I think that it is also right to adopt what I would call the bountiful eye of grace: searching for everything that is good in the life of European Christians in terms of generosity, even if it is only the "day of small things" not to be despised (Zechariah 4:10) or the "bruised reed" that the servant of the Lord will not break (Isaiah 42:3). If we do this, I guess that we will find that there are more Christians living something of the reality of a truly Christ-centered generosity than we would have imagined. They have not waited for us to tell them to be generous, even if they may not have an articulated holistic theology including generosity as a crucial part of discipleship! When you come to know them, you realize that they are able to give a lot, be it money, time, hospitality, or practical help. Some with rather modest income will be very much willing to share what they have with the poor. Some of them will be challenging the consumerist Western mentality by very simple but significant acts, such as asking their relatives not to give them anything for Christmas or their birthday and instead to make a donation to a Christian charity.

---

8. Some of them also contribute to the work of secular charitable organizations.

But maybe their generosity is exercised in the daily routine of ordinary life, doesn't show any heroic marks, and cannot be told in a dramatic story that will raise enthusiasm in the listeners. It is still real. This kind of generosity will be found in churches of Western Europe (and all over the world). It is often fragile and threatened specifically by the culture of covetousness or more globally by what Jesus called "the worries of this life and the deceitfulness of wealth" (Matthew 13:22). It can be mixed with some unpleasant trends indicating this, but it is there—precious and a blessing in the lives of those who benefit from it. I would plead that the one who has eyes to see would notice the signs of encouragement.

This being said, we should also stress the fact that Christ-centered generosity is countercultural in contemporary Western Europe and becomes increasingly so as time goes by. This is because God is less and less recognized as Creator, let alone as the ultimate owner of everything; because Christ and the grace of God in Him is less and less known and understood; because money is such a powerful idol in European countries nowadays; and because the standards of success in life have little to do with being a faithful steward. These realities put real pressure on individual Christians, families, and churches.

Generosity and Self-Fulfillment

The biblical call to generosity is linked with a vision for the future that gives it a kind of priority (1 Timothy 6:17–19), but in contemporary Western Europe, "the life that is truly life" is deemed to be the present life and instead of working to "store treasures in heaven" (Matthew 6:20), the ideal seems to be "I want it all, and I want it now!" It should be stressed not only that Westerners do not think seriously about the coming age (which is common to them and to most sinners, whatever their culture), but also that their earthly hopes for the future or the next generations are becoming unstable or even insignificant. All this tends to make people more self-centered, and I am afraid that the measure of self-centeredness that Christians are prone to indulge in is growing. It does not necessarily kill every form of generosity, but it weakens the

Christ-centered character of generosity and can lock Christians in the "chains" mentioned in Part I—pride, power, praise—and maybe one more: generosity as a means of self-fulfillment.

Western contemporary culture does not encourage individuals to be generous because of the consumerist lifestyle that it promotes. Consumerism prompts people, including Christians, to become entangled in debt, which is a concrete obstacle to their being generous, at least with their money. They really cannot afford to give much to the church, to Christian ministries, or to the poor. Even without that, many borrow their ideas as to what their living standards should be from the society around them, and it puts serious limitations on their ability to give. Randy Alcorn is right when he writes that "one of our central spiritual decisions is determining what is a reasonable amount to live on."[9] Christians in Western Europe should indeed think more consciously about this matter as a decision they have to take on spiritual grounds and not accept what broader society thinks is the norm. This might mean adopting a more realistic outlook on the rationale for our spending and pondering more seriously questions such as: Do I need this? Is it really useful? Will it foster my family life or other healthy relationships? Or does my desire to consume this product or buy this item reveal that I am not able to find my satisfaction and security in God and that, therefore, I am looking for something else or something more?[10] I would argue that the spiritual steps we need to take again and again will lead us to these three things: first, learning contentment even with little ("If we have food and clothing, we will be content with that," 1 Timothy 6:8); second, truly enjoying what God gives us ("Who richly provides us with everything for our enjoyment," 6:17); and third, "to be generous and willing to share" (6:18). Although this last clause is specifically addressed to "those who are rich in this present world," it can find an application in the life of everyone and is very relevant to Western Christians!

9. Randy Alcorn, *The Treasure Principle: Discovering the Secret of Joyful Giving* (Colorado Springs: Multnomah Books, 2001), 27.

10. One can find further useful thinking in Tim Chester, *Good News to the Poor: Sharing the Gospel through Social Involvement* (Leicester: IVP, 2004), ch. 7.

The tax system can also influence issues of generosity in Europe, first of all because state welfare organizes a kind of collective generosity both inside a country and abroad (official development assistance), contributing to the feeling that the state has the primary responsibility in sharing the wealth and providing for the needy, not the individual. A second issue is this: donations to churches or Christian NGOs are often eligible for to tax deductions. While I cannot find anything wrong in this, I am afraid that in some cases the amount of nondeductible money that Christians become willing to give might be (much?) smaller than we would imagine. Maybe Christian churches and ministries will have some very bad surprises on the day the governments cut the possibility of tax-deductible receipts for donors.[11]

The European context thus confronts us with challenges, temptations, and opportunities. Christians are trying to find their way in the midst of this "covetous society." Even if some of them are doing quite well, we still need to ask how we can move together toward a more generous lifestyle.

Toward a More Generous Lifestyle

Isaiah 58 presents the picture of a self-centered people preoccupied by its own business, oppressing vulnerable people, and complaining that God does not notice them when they fast. But the answer from the prophet is to become God-centered by delighting in the Sabbath and be open to the need of your neighbor, especially the poor and the crushed down. In *58: The Film*, Pastor Chris Durso challenges his audience with these words:

> Some of you have been calling out to God for so long, and you've been wondering why He hasn't responded, because He wanted you to step out, put your own insecurities, doubts, hurts, and pain aside and fight someone else's battle, go on somebody else's behalf and pray for them. Because He promises—if you pray for them, then He

---

11. See my "From Whom Can Christian Agencies Ask for Money?" *The New Urban World Journal*, no. 2 (November 2013): 67–69.

will meet you. If you go to somebody else with the stuff that they're dealing with, you will see His glory come forth in your own life. [12]

We, Western European Christians, need to realize that there are a lot of unsolved problems in our life *and that we should not wait for them to be solved before we start being generous.* Our priority in life is often to put an end to that which hurts us. The rest can come later. But God's priorities are different: He wants us to love Him with all our heart and to love our neighbor as ourselves. Maybe this is one of the reasons why helping the poor is a central issue linked with generosity: the poor are precisely the ones who are not able to give something equivalent in return (Luke 14:12–14). The one who genuinely cares for them will have to abandon self-centeredness.

Pastor Oral Hatava, who contributed to the launching of an abiding work with children (many of them refugees) in Paris, stresses that true generosity doesn't pay attention to what the person can give to me in return. Even the joy of giving, he says, must be seen as a collateral blessing and not the reason why I share. [13] His initiative is inspiring in that it offers opportunities to exercise generosity at different levels and is well fitted to the local context: Christians in Paris (some of whom have very real hardships to go through) would be able, for example, to offer a better Christmas to children with (much) worse living conditions than they have simply by volunteering their time, talent, or creativity ,or by giving money. Not everyone has the ability to start a new generosity initiative, but everyone with eyes to see will have opportunities to do good and be generous. But it will mean accepting to care for the needs of others while our own needs are not completely met yet.

Whom Do We Belong To?

Scott Rodin's contribution has pointed to God as being the ultimate owner

---

12. This forty-minute film can be seen on www.live58.org. The website includes material on generosity and fighting against poverty.

13. See Oral Hatava, "La joie passe-t-elle par le passage?" *SEL*: http://selfrance.org/uploads /media/Joie_et_partage.pdf, accessed February 27, 2014.

of everything and to the motto "It's all His!" I'd like to stress one aspect of this affirmation that is especially relevant to the European context. If we are to learn to be stewards of what God has entrusted to us, we have first to rediscover this simple truth: *we do not belong to ourselves*. One of the greatest lies that Europeans believe today, regarding what Scott Rodin calls the "spirit of property," has to do with themselves.

As John M. Frame rightly remarks, the Bible affirms private property: "The eighth commandment, 'you shall not steal' (Exodus 20:15), assumes that although all things belong ultimately to God, he has made a difference between what belongs to me and what belongs to you."[14] So there is a sense in which our money or material possessions do belong to us, even if God is their ultimate owner. There may be a sense in which our body, our time, or even our life belongs to us, but it seems to be less clear.

In his famous *Screwtape Letters*, C. S. Lewis has a fascinating chapter on property that deserves a full quote.[15] Screwtape, the tempter, writes to the apprentice regarding the man he is supposed to lead into sin: "You must therefore zealously guard in his mind the curious assumption 'My time is my own.' Let him have the feeling that he starts each day as the lawful possessor of twenty-four hours." But he adds a little later, "You have here a delicate task. The assumption which you want him to go on making is so absurd that, if once it is questioned, even we cannot find a shred of argument in its defense." The demon continues stating that the "sense of ownership in general is always to be encouraged," while, in reality, "the word 'Mine' in its fully possessive sense cannot be uttered by a human being about anything."[16]

It is difficult to overstate the extent to which typical Western people believe that they belong to themselves, with their bodies and their time. It has a frightening bearing on issues such as abortion, euthanasia, suicide,

---

14. John M. Frame, "The Bible and Joe the Plumber": http://www.frame-poythress.org/the-bible-and-joe-the-plumber/, accessed January 22, 2014. I would not necessarily endorse the economic model that John Frame thinks he can derive from the Bible.

15. This fictional book is composed of letters from Screwtape, expert tempter (a demon) to his nephew (a novice tempter).

16. C. S. Lewis, *The Screwtape Letters* (New York: Bantam Books, 1982), 95–99 (letter XXI).

and sexual sins, but it also breeds less spectacular sins—sometimes just as harmful—such as selfishness and lack of generosity. This mentality infects to some extent the thinking and behavior of Christians.

Both by right of creation and of redemption, Christians do not belong to themselves. The New Testament probably insists more on redemption and the cost it involved: we have been bought with the precious blood of Christ so that we should belong to Him (1 Corinthians 6:19b–20a). Nevertheless, the global picture that the Bible provides us with to structure our thinking and living begins with creation. Seeing ourselves and others—and indeed the rest of the world!—as created, if pondered seriously, changes everything. Whatever else we may rightly say about any human being or any part of the world, one thing is always sure and fundamental: this person or this thing is part of God's creation and therefore belongs to Him by an absolute right. God created the world *ex nihilo* (from nothing). This implies that He owes nothing to anybody and doesn't have to share His right of ownership of anything: "Who has ever given to God, that God should repay them?" (Romans 11:35). We, on the other hand, receive everything from Him (including our very being and every breath of life we take) and owe everything to Him.

It is useful to denounce the idolatry of money; it is also useful to stress our vocation as stewards of what ultimately (in the "fully possessive" sense, as C. S. Lewis has it) belongs to God. But here I would suggest that Western Christians specifically need to come to a fresh realization of the Lord's ownership of their being, life, and time (Romans 14:7–9; 1 Corinthians 6:19b–20a). It also has a powerful liberating potential: if God owns me, He is the one in charge of me and I can be open to the needs of the church, mission, those who suffer hardship, the poor... As Jesus says in Matthew 25:40: "Whatever you did for one of the least of these brothers and sisters of mine, you did for me."

To achieve these changes of mentality in the hearts and lives of Western Christians, we have to face a double challenge: rooting generosity in the grace of God and giving practical teaching and direction on generosity.

Giving and Grace

The Heidelberg Catechism, one of the best-known texts of the sixteenth-century Protestant Reformation, begins thus:

> What is thy only comfort in life and death?
>
> That I with body and soul, both in life and death, am not my own, but belong unto my faithful Saviour Jesus Christ; who, with his precious blood, has fully satisfied for all my sins, and delivered me from all the power of the devil; and so preserves me that without the will of my heavenly Father, not a hair can fall from my head; yea, that all things must be subservient to my salvation, and therefore, by his Holy Spirit, He also assures me of eternal life, and makes me sincerely willing and ready, henceforth, to live unto him. [17]

The Catechism very interestingly starts with the bold statement "I am not my own!" (a statement on property!) and links it with the grace of Christ, "my faithful Saviour." Generous living should be seen as part of that life unto God, mentioned at the end of the first answer, and as flowing from that personal application to myself of the grace of God who saved me and keeps me safe in His hand.

It is vital that preachers insist more on grace and specifically on satisfaction for sins, justification by faith, adoption, and so forth in their teaching if we really want to see more Christ-centered generosity in our churches. No significant steps will be achieved toward this purpose without more powerful preaching on grace and how a new life of generosity is articulated by it. [18] It is free grace that produces fruits in the lives of those who receive it.

---

17. Quoted after the version found on http://www.ccel.org/creeds/heidelberg-cat.html, accessed January 23, 2014.

18. For more on this, see my "Responsible Generosity," *Evangelical Review of Theology* 37, no.1 (2013): 34–45 and my "La responsabilité sociale des chrétiens," *Réseau FEF Infos* 136 (2013): 4–11 (especially 7–8).

Practical Teaching and Direction

Practical teaching should be connected with the preaching of grace. It will urge Christians to care for their neighbor even when these Christians must face unsolved problems in their own lives; it will try to lead them to realize more and more that "with body and soul, both in life and death" they are not their own but belong to Jesus Christ. Can we point to concrete practical steps that could be taken to achieve this purpose? Let me suggest one or two, among many possibilities.

In 2009, the Church of England issued a booklet called *Giving for Life: Encouraging Generosity in Your Parish.*[19] It provides practical advice on how to encourage generosity by teaching generous giving, by linking giving to mission and ministry, by providing an annual review of giving, and by thanking givers. The initiative could be inspiring in several respects. It could prompt churches, denominations, Christian alliances, Christian networks, businesses, etc., to take a stand on issues such as giving and generosity; supporting churches, ministries, and mission agencies; and working with the poor, etc. The more Christian leaders and representative bodies are able to speak with one voice and effectively communicate on these topics, the more it is likely that a culture of generosity can be fostered among Christians.

Generosity is not to be seen as another activity that Christians and churches are to try to add to an already very busy schedule. Neither should it be seen only as a Christian value that ought to be encouraged nor as the craze of one or two original folks trying to share their concern with others. It should rather be a culture to Christians—that is, a kind of second nature. Christian fellowship, which includes sharing material possessions, is a normal part of church life (Acts 2:42) and alms-giving a normal part of a disciple's lifestyle (Matthew 6:1–4). What a pity if we are not able to have a common voice on a subject such as this!

The content of such a common message should be both challenging and encouraging. It should be very respectful of everyone's choices but

---

19. It is available online: http://www.parishresources.org.uk/wp-content/uploads/GfL_pcc_guide.pdf, accessed January 23, 2014.

present unequivocally the teaching of the scriptures on money. It should be concrete but not provide a detailed rule that every individual should follow by necessity. It should also give some examples either providing inspiration (not necessarily to be slavishly copied) or concrete choices that one could make (for example, presenting causes that need to be funded or volunteering opportunities).

Is it possible to do this? I think it is. One could find some examples of this in *Lifestyle in the Eighties: An Evangelical Commitment to Simple Lifestyle*.[20] One thought-provoking sentence in this text is that "those of us who belong to the West need the help of our Third World brothers and sisters in evaluating our standards of spending." Whatever we might think of this precise suggestion, let me state that I think that we have something to learn and to receive from people living in poverty (especially—though not exclusively—Christian brothers and sisters) on issues such as sharing, generosity, and contentment.[21] Working as I do in a Christian organization supporting local partners in developing countries in their fight against poverty, one of the most inspiring parts of my job has been the opportunity to meet brothers and sisters from the South showing me the beauty of costly involvement with the poor.

Much of the Anglican booklet could also be reused with little adaptation in countries other than England and/or other denominational and church structure contexts. Furthermore, it could provide the opportunity for useful discussions. Many churches and leaders would teach or encourage tithing and giving voluntary offerings, with tithes being dedicated exclusively to the local church. *Giving for Life* has the thought-provoking suggestion that Christians give 5 percent to the church and 5 percent more to "other work that helps to build God's kingdom." It is challenging both to people who give much less than this percentage and to churches and leaders who would not have dreamed of Christians giving that proportion

20. Ronald J. Sider, ed., *Lifestyle in the Eighties: An Evangelical Commitment to Simple Lifestyle* (Philadelphia: The Westminster Press, 1982), 13–19.

21. See my "Être à l'écoute des pauvres et apprendre d'eux : quelques perspectives bibliques" on http://www.selfrance.org/uploads/media/Reflexions_-_Daniel_Hillion__BD_.pdf, accessed January 31, 2014.

to parachurch entities. I will not try to discuss this particular issue here, but I think it should be reflected upon, and I would even add that we should ask the question whether we should not encourage Christians to exercise (Christ-centered!) generosity even toward secular organizations contributing to the common good.[22]

Conclusion

There is still a long way to go on the journey of the faithful steward for Western Christians, but there is hope if only the free grace of God will be preached more powerfully and linked with the new life that is to flow from it. The European context is not especially conducive to a culture of generosity, but Christians should take this as an opportunity to live counterculturally and to show how the grace of God can change a human heart and community. If we do this, it will surely benefit the church, the mission, the poor, and many who are in need.

Questions for Individual Reflection and Discussion in Small Groups

- Give examples of the way in which a "covetous society" or a consumerist lifestyle puts limits on generosity. Discuss how the message in some advertisements goes counter to a culture of generosity.[23]
- What small but concrete steps can be taken to go against this general trend?
- Have you ever met Christians whose discreet generosity in ordinary life has impressed you? How could it inspire you to be generous in your own way? Do you think that Christians from the South could also inspire you in the area of generosity? How?

---

22. Randy Alcorn seems to discourage this on the grounds that "for every good secular organization there's a Christian organization doing the same work—but with an eternal perspective." See *The Treasure Principle*, 89. The argument has real weight, but it leaves me uneasy. There certainly is room for Christian organizations (I am actually employed by one of them!), but Christians are not called to withdraw from the world in a kind of evangelical ghetto. There is also room for Christian involvement within and for the benefit of good secular organizations.

23. More on this in Chester, *Good News to the Poor*, ch. 7.

- Do you think that by managing your money differently, you would be able to be more generous? If so, what prevents you from doing it?
- How do you think that the message of grace and the daily experience of living God's grace could impact generous living? What can you do to expose yourself again and again to the grace of God?

Generosity on the Receiving End, from Hosts to Guests

By Dr. Wei-Leong Goh (Singapore)

HealthServe is a community health clinic that was birthed over coffee sessions with a dear friend. For six months, we discussed everything from the state of the world to local church and mission challenges. We felt impressed that migration and poverty were key elements in our new mission field. Starting a community clinic staffed mainly by unpaid medical personnel seemed, then, the natural response to what we perceived was underway—migrant workers were fast transforming Singapore's urban landscape.

The clinic was our point of entry into Singapore's red-light district, Geylang, where major global issues inevitably collided amidst Chinese, Indian, Bangladeshi, and Burmese laborers. Through much experimentation and failure, we evolved and added a free legal clinic, social assistance, and a food program. Then God sent Mr. Yin to challenge us in an unexpected way.

Mr. Yin came from Shandong, China, after paying 40,000 renminbi (RMB; approximately $6,500 USD) to a Chinese employment agent. In Singapore, for three months, he earned barely $15 USD/day as a construction worker in a lift shaft before unfortunately losing most of his hearing. Deaf, unemployed, penniless, and homeless, Yin wandered the streets of Geylang until three sympathetic streetwalkers gave him money for food. They then directed him to HealthServe Community Clinic.

Yin became a member of our loving community, where his hearing problems were treated by volunteer specialists and friends. At the same time, he also embraced a newfound faith in Jesus Christ. After a lengthy twelve-month wait, Yin received his workers' compensation. Just before returning to China, he approached me wanting to give the ministry a substantial percentage of the money he had been paid. I vehemently refused until he said, "Unless you accept my money, I am not a part of this community. Besides, if you are my brother, you must accept this gift."

We accepted the gift.

Receiving, I realized, did not come as easily as giving. Prior to receiving Yin as a brother, we had been giving: food, water, love, hope, courage, medicine, perspective, insight, and legal aid. We thought this was community.

We didn't understand that community in its fullness constitutes more than just giving. It was only in receiving that we allowed Yin and many others after him to truly become part of a whole and generous community. Mr. Yin was affirmed as a brother in Christ when he was allowed to meaningfully contribute, and this act simultaneously helped him discover his identity in Christ and the dynamism of his faith.

When we accepted his money, it was a major paradigm shift for us because we had been so accustomed to helping others and never needing help. We felt vulnerable but liberated from the shackles of a patronizing NGO. We learned that while we are usually hosts, we too can be blessed by becoming guests. Our ability to receive gives recognition and restores dignity to those we help.

Yin has since returned to China. He owns a small, successful barbershop and actively participates in a local house church. HealthServe, now more deeply relational, happily celebrates generosity in its entirety—both as host and guest!

Learning Generosity through My Parents' Example

By Frances Ann Heald (United States)

As long as I can remember, I've watched my parents and my grandparents give. I grew up with giving all around me. When I was seven, we did the Crown Financial program for kids, so we were splitting our allowance into giving, saving, and spending, and we would always get to decide where we wanted to give our money. That was always really exciting to talk through with my dad.

My parents exposed me to giving early on, and I like to say that they helped me understand the concept of giving before I even understood the concept of money. In fourth grade, at the age of ten, I went on a trip with my dad, and I was sitting safely by his side in a taxi as we drove from the Mumbai airport to our hotel. As I looked out the car window, I saw a toddler on the street. She was on the sidewalk and was covered with a newspaper; that's all she had. There was no attentive mother standing over her, no protective father keeping watch—it was just her, just by herself.

Returning to the safety of my home on Lookout Mountain became the hardest part of traveling. I returned feeling depressed, upset, and hopeless. I was not prepared for what I had seen. My dad promised God that he would take me on two trips every year, so since then I have been to over twenty different countries. A lot of these countries were very poor countries, and we were seeing things that were beyond anything that my peers had seen.

Before many of the trips, I prayed that God would open my eyes, but I was not prepared for the suffering I would see and the guilt I would feel because of that. I began to tell my parents about my struggle with what I

53

had seen, and one of the things my dad realized was that I needed more time to process. I was going back home to school and was surrounded by friends who knew little of what I had seen. Well, he went straight to work talking with all of these different ministries that we had seen at work in these countries.

So, through processing with my dad, I was able to see the hope for God's promise to restore all things. The truth is constantly setting me free from the suffering and the depression that I felt because of that.

One experience God used to help me understand generosity was my family's decision to start an adoption process. At every orphanage I had visited, my sister and I would come up to my dad bringing kids. We were holding sometimes, like, two or three at a time, and we would be like, "Dad, can we please take them home? I can buy them a one-way ticket! I have the money in my bank account." And he'd say, "No, no, we can't do that." But we were persistent. We would write letters and talk about it all the time. My sister would even send him Happy Adoption Day cards. And so after four years of pleading, our parents gave us our Christmas present in 2005, and that was to start the adoption process.

I'd never understood the concept of being adopted into God's family until we got LeeLee. She's not an extra part of our family, she's not an extension, she is family. There's no difference in the way I look at her and the way I look at all my other adopted siblings and all my other biological siblings. It was then that I realized that God doesn't look at me any differently. He looks at me as not an addition to his family but as a child who was always meant to be there.

Since LeeLee's adoption in 2007, we have also adopted Lucy and Bella. About two days after we came home with Lucy in August, we planned on going to visit our farm. My dad came up to Lucy and said, "Lucy, did you know you have a farm? You have horses and a lake. It's gonna be so much fun." As I listened to my dad tell Lucy about her farm, I couldn't help but think about how excited God gets when we're adopted into his family. It's like He's saying, "I cannot wait for you to see what I have for you. Everything I have is yours."

When Lucy became a part of our family, everything that we had became hers. She did nothing to merit what she got. It was freely given to her. My adopted sisters were completely hopeless. They had nothing, and they had no way of saving themselves. There was nothing they could do to get them out of the situation they were in. It was only by the generosity of Christ, through my parents, that they received what they have now. God showed me that the same is true for me and the rest of my family. We did nothing to deserve what we have.

I give glory to Christ because I am blessed beyond all measure to get to take part in the work that He is doing to restore brokenness in the world through my family. I've seen my sister go from a malnourished seventeen-month-old with clubbed feet and double hip dysplasia to a firecracker of a seven-year-old racing down the mountain on skis. And I've seen Lucy go from speaking only a few Mandarin words to singing "Jesus Loves Me." I realized my parents received the greatest return of all. They invested 100 percent into eight little lives and received life to the fullest.

Kingdom-Focused Generosity: Strategic Generosity to Reach the Least and Lost

BY PAT MURDOCK (UNITED STATES)

Today there are 2.3 billion believers who call themselves followers of Jesus. There are 5 million churches, 43,000 denominations, and over 12 million full-time Christian workers, yet 99.7 percent of all ministry financial support goes to building and maintaining the existing church. Only 0.3 percent is spent on extending the reach of the church.

What about the Lord's Great Commission? His command is clear: "Go and make disciples of *all* nations" (Matthew 28:19, emphasis mine).

What is our progress? Have we been obedient?

At this point, there are still four thousand languages with no written or oral scriptures, three thousand people groups with no missionaries, over 1 million villages with no churches, and 3.5 billion Muslims, Buddhists, Hindus, and secularists without Christ.

Why hasn't every people group been reached? How can you make your life Count for Zero, so that one day there will be:

- Zero languages without the scriptures,
- Zero people groups without disciple-makers,
- Zero people who have not heard the gospel,
- Zero oral learners without an oral Bible, and
- Zero villages or neighborhoods without a church.

It is said in 1 Chronicles 12:32 that the men of Issachar "understood the times and knew what Israel should do." It is time for a new generation of Issachar leaders, men and women who understand the times and know from scriptures what needs to be done to finish the Great Commission.

The Lord has shown you great favor. He has given you a voice of influence and a global calling in this generation for His kingdom purposes.

Because of your leadership in the battle for the souls of all people, please consider how you can use the time, talent, treasure, networks, and truth that God has entrusted to you toward the fulfillment of the most important assignment that our Lord Jesus left to you and to me, to "go and make disciples of all nations."

Give Hope: A Legacy of Giving Back in the US

BY CARLETTE PATTERSON (UNITED STATES)

Our lives are about the choices we make. Once we make a choice, the details of that choice begin to create our lives. Small choices, big choices, and how we handle the details of each choice begin to complete the pages of our life story.

Some choices, just like some chapters in our life story, seem irrelevant. And then there are moments when we make a choice and later realize that choice was a life changer.

Steve Patterson played professional basketball in the United States. But beyond that, he learned generosity through life choices. In 2004, Steve's life on earth ended. He was fifty-six years old and had been diagnosed with cancer just a few weeks prior to his death. Steve's story ended quickly, without notice. Because Steve had chosen God, his life began on the same day it ended. What Steve did not know was that every time he had the courage to honor the quiet whisper of God telling him to do for others, he was playing a small role in something so much bigger than himself.

Two men had a great influence on Steve's being ready to become a champion. One was his father, and the other was his Sunday school teacher and high school coach, Bob McCutcheon. If those two men had not chosen to live by faith and to give generously of their time, Steve would not have had the choices he had for his life.

It was through his father that Steve learned of salvation through the grace of God. It was Bob McCutcheon who first told Steve of all the potential he had and the vast horizon that lay before him. The combination of these two men prepared Steve to accept the desire that God

59

placed on his heart. He wanted to be a champion—not just in sports but also in life.

God prepared Steve for His purpose, to use the platform that his talents provided for him to share the gospel. Steve's father and Bob McCutcheon prepared Steve to play for legendary basketball coach John Wooden. Coach Wooden prepared Steve to be a champion in basketball. The choices Steve made day by day made him a champion in life.

He achieved his goals of playing in the NBA, becoming a basketball coach, and owning a business. By the world's standards, he was a champion. Yet in his heart, he did not feel like a champion. Something was missing.

Steve began to search back over his life story, a story that started with a father-son relationship. It was then that Steve discovered that it was only through a Father-Son relationship that life could truly be won. The details of how to be a champion in life were clearly demonstrated by Jesus doing as His father asked him to do.

It is love that makes a champion. God loved us enough to send His only son to save us. Jesus loved his father enough to suffer, sacrifice, and be crucified for us. How could we ever show our love to a Father and Son that chose us? We can follow their example. We can choose love.

If Steve rewrote his life story based on love, it would read something like this: love of sports led to a life of blessings; love of God provided meaning to life's questions; loving others—giving back—added purpose to every choice.

God's plan for how we can give back is written in the pages of our life story. It is in the simple, quiet moments when we do something that seems irrelevant, and then, without our knowing, His glory is revealed, and someone we don't even know now has a chance to experience God's love.

Steve's story has continued to be written years after he put down the pen. He has been honored with an award given in his name as an example of how to be a champion in sports and life—the Steve Patterson Award for Excellence in Sports Philanthropy. The award is not about Steve Patterson; the award represents what Steve did with the life God gave him.

Coach Wooden was a firm believer in preparation and practice. He would tell his players, "If you practice, your time will come. If you don't practice, your time will come and you won't be ready." We know our time will come when this "game of life" ends. Will you be ready to stand before God and watch your game film of what you did play-by-play, day by day, with the gifts He chose to give you? Are you utilizing your daily practice time for His glory or yours? What would our life be like if every day while we practiced our faith, we gave hope generously to the people that God chose to place in our life for a moment, a day, or even a lifetime?

Coach Wooden told his players, "Don't measure yourself by what you have accomplished, but by what you should have accomplished with your ability." God has blessed each one of us abundantly with talents designed to G.I.V.E.H.O.P.E (Get Involved, Volunteer, Educate, Help Other People Everyday).

To win we must lose ourselves. Life is not about what we do or what we accomplish—it is about Jesus. Every day we are blessed with the choice to live by faith, to give hope, and to cherish and receive love. And the greatest of these is love—His love for us, our love for others, and how this combination gives people the choice of eternity. How would your life story read if you rewrote it based on love? Who would you want to give back to as a way of honoring all that God has given you? How could you be as generous to others as God has been to you?

PART III

Living Generously in an African Culture

By Rev. Dennis Tongoi (Kenya)

hrist-centered generosity was described in Part I of this book as being predicated on the fact that we own nothing—all belongs to God, and we are stewards. Christ-centered generosity is distinguished from philanthropy in that it is motivated by obedience to Christ and an attitude of joyfulness, not just a response to human needs. Everyone can live generously irrespective of whatever kind of resources they manage. Jesus expected as much from the person given one talent as he did from the one given five (Matthew 25:26–27). For those in Africa, the majority who live in humble circumstances can live just as generously as those who have plenty.

In this section we shall look at the source, motivation, and obstacles to living generously. Generosity has been defined as "the quality of being kind, understanding, and not selfish: the quality of being generous; especially: willingness to give money and other valuable things to others."[24] In this chapter I will be using the word "generous" or its derivatives interchangeably with its synonyms, such as "giving."

Living Generously Reflects to the World the God We Serve

God's kindness is to the just and the unjust, as we see in Matthew 5:45. God's mercies to the undeserving and God's goodness to all are themes that cut across both the Old and New Testaments. These reach a climax in John 3:16 when we read, "For God so loved the world that he gave

---

24. *Merriam-Webster Online*, s.v. "generosity," accessed December 22, 2014, http://www.merriam-webster.com/dictionary/generosity.

his one and only Son…." A life of generosity by followers of Jesus Christ models this key attribute of God's nature to others who do not know Him. Generosity was one of the first characteristics of the early church, whose members shared everything, not calling anything their own, as in Acts 4:32. As a result of God's Spirit at work in them, people became more important than things, and building relationships was given priority, as they ate from house to house. This acceptance and receiving of God's unconditional and unmerited love motivated the early church to live and respond generously to one another. People who have not experienced God's love or surrendered to His reign over their lives are in danger of the bondage of pride, power, and praise discussed in Part I on one extreme. On the other extreme, the danger is of a victim mentality, where they are unable to see God's abundant provision already supplied, as in the case of many communities in Africa that live in poverty in the midst of plenty.

Generosity is a reflection of the freedom that comes from being in Christ and overcoming the self-centered bondage of the sinful nature and learning to love our neighbor as ourselves, as in Galatians 5:13–15. Africans place a higher value on the community than they do on the individual. This has both strengths and challenges. Strengths in that sharing of material things is almost expected, sometimes even demanded. Weakness in that this could result in sharing our resources that include time and space in a grudging or dutiful manner and not in the way of an obedient and joyful steward that exemplifies the Christ-centered generosity defined in Part I.

Generosity Is More than Money

Generosity is a willingness to share what has been entrusted to us in obedient response to God's love. A generous life is not based on how much one has or does not have; it is not only for those who have surplus. The churches in Macedonia illustrate this truth. The apostle Paul, writing about the churches in Macedonia in 2 Corinthians 8:1–5, tells of how, despite their severe trial and poverty, they "urgently pleaded" for the opportunity to give to the needs of their fellow believers in Jerusalem who were very needy as a result of severe drought. Paul tells us that these Macedonians first of all gave themselves to the Lord before giving for the needs of the saints in Jerusalem. Generosity is demonstrated in this case as giving of oneself, not just of one's possessions. The story is told of a wealthy woman in a community who would always send large checks to support those in her community who had been bereaved, but she herself would never show up or participate in the hard work of serving the guests at the funeral wake. When she in turn had a death in her family, the other women sent her several checks, but none of them showed up to mourn with her or serve her guests at the funeral. She realized how poor she was relationally despite her money.

Generosity is more than giving money; it is giving oneself. The churches in Macedonia did not give out of a surplus but gave because God's grace was at work in their lives. On the contrary, Paul tells us of their being tested by many troubles and being very poor. But we see them giving "as much as they were able, and even beyond their ability." God's grace transforms us from being self-centered people to being other-centered. Self-centeredness is characterized by greed and accumulation—as earlier stated, the desire for control. Other-centeredness results in service and generosity. Unlike other gods who demand sacrifice, God, the creator of all that is both seen and unseen, is a generous God who sacrificed His own son Jesus Christ so as to reconcile this fallen creation back to Himself, as we see in Colossians 1:15–20. African cultures have a rich heritage that values solidarity, or *ubuntu*, as it is known in southern Africa. This is demonstrated in times of celebration, such as weddings or childbirth, and times of sorrow, such as illness or funerals, when we carry the load together by not arriving empty-handed.

Generosity as an Antidote to Greed

As a result of Adam and Eve's disobedience in the Book of Genesis, humanity experienced a broken relationship with God, fellow humans, and God's creation. As a result of mankind's isolation from God, Romans 1:21–23 shows us that self became more important than others and idolatry replaced the worship of the creator God. Poverty was the final result. This poverty manifests itself in two extremes. First, there's poverty of being, where we have a diminished view of ourselves and others and we prioritize the accumulation of material possessions at the expense of our well-being, as these become the means of our identity. Second, there is material poverty, where passivity overrides personal responsibility and we do nothing to address our needs, blaming others or waiting for others to intervene in our circumstances.

Those who are rich are not always generous. A family may progress economically and move from a condition of lack or poverty to surplus, perhaps due to moving to the city from the village or becoming successful in their careers or businesses. The temptation is to be less, not more, generous. Paul tells Timothy in 1 Timothy 6:17–19 to help those who are "rich in this present world" to beware of the temptation to pride and idolatry that places trust in money rather than God. Such people are urged to be "rich in good deeds, and to be generous and willing to share." Generosity destroys the stronghold of idolatry, which is often driven by self-centered greed or the desire to accumulate for oneself. In Luke 12:13–20, Jesus tells of a rich farmer who was very successful in his farming, but this success was very self-centered. The man is called a fool for assuming that the quality and longevity of his life was related to how much he had accumulated. Jesus gives a stern warning on the need to be aware of greed in our life.

In Matthew 6:24, Jesus tells his disciples that one can only serve one master at a time—either God or money but not both. Generosity allows us to break the bondage caused by greed and be freed to respond joyfully to the opportunities that God has designed for us to serve His purposes as we let Him be the ruler and controller of our life. In this way we are contributing to the furtherance of God's kingdom (His rule) over Satan's control in the spiritual battle, described in Part I as the battle between love for God and love for money.

Generosity Can Be Abused

Greed is a big problem that all people must avoid. Leaders need to be an example of generosity and not greed. Church leaders too can be tempted to be greedy, especially those who have fruitful ministries. In 2 Kings 5:20–26, we read of one such story in the Old Testament where Elisha's servant, Gehazi, is tempted to deceive Naaman, a wealthy Aramean army commander who has been healed of leprosy through Elisha's ministry. Elisha has refused to accept any gift for this miraculous healing. Gehazi, however, goes behind Elisha's back and lies to Naaman that his master has an unexpected need. He fraudulently accepts a gift from Naaman. When Elisha finds out, Gehazi and his descendants are cursed to suffer from leprosy forever. Naaman in this case is very generous, but Gehazi, a spiritual leader, exploits this generosity for personal gain.

Leaders too can be exploited in their generosity. In John 13:8–10, John writes of Jesus's attempt to serve his disciples by washing their feet. Peter at first declines and says, "You shall never wash my feet." But Jesus reminds him of his need to be washed clean in order to be part of Christ. Peter then tells Jesus, "Not just my feet but my hands and my head as well." Jesus declines and tells Peter that a person who has had a bath needs only wash his feet. Jesus meets the needs and not the wants of Peter. Christ-centered generosity avoids the temptation to respond to the needs of those we serve with the wrong motive or to be exploited by those we serve. This danger is particularly true of leaders in Africa, where there are so many obvious material needs that are easier to respond to than the spiritual, social, or physiological needs of those we serve.

Generosity requires discernment. In Numbers 7:3–9 we see Moses exercising discernment as he distributes resources to the Levitical clans for work at the tabernacle. He has received twelve oxen and six covered carts from leaders of other clans. The Merarite clan leaders receive twice as many as the Gershonites, but the Kohathites receive none. He distributes these "as each man's work requires." The Kohathites do not need any because God had commanded them to carry their things on their shoulders. Generosity is part of our stewardship, and we need to prayerfully align our giving decisions in light of God's kingdom priorities. In some situations, one may not have to give anything material if that is what will advance God's purposes in the situation. In Acts 3:6, the apostles

Peter and John did not have silver and gold but were able to pray for the paralytic to walk again—a far more valuable gift.

Leaders can foster generosity by being good models to their followers. In Acts 20:35 the apostle Paul, at the end of his ministry in Ephesus, tells of how he worked with his hands to provide not only for his own needs but also for those of his companions, saying, "It is more blessed to give than to receive." Here we see a leader setting the example of generous living, not just expecting it from his followers.

In 1 Chronicles 29:1–11, we read of another leader who models generosity. King David sets the pace and prepares for the reign of Solomon, who is to succeed him as king. King David gives all his private treasures of gold and silver for the construction of the temple. The other leaders imitate this act of generosity. In the end the people rejoice at the generosity of their leaders, and everyone is filled with joy.

Living Generously Reflects Our Relationship with God

Generosity is part of the larger picture of stewardship, the management of time, treasure, and talents that are all gifts from God.

Generosity in our worship is a reflection of our relationship with God (Proverbs 3:9– 10; Malachi 3:10) and opens the way for us to continue to experience His increased abundance in all areas of our life. Malachi 1:6–9, 13–14 shows us that holding back in our worship through giving can be an indication of a diminishing relationship with God.

In Africa there is a tendency to assume that all generous people are godly or have a relationship with God. Political leaders who become very generous in doing "God's work" especially around election time can exploit this perception for personal gain. Generosity, however, does not reflect whether or not a person knows God. The opportunity exists to invite such people who may give for the wrong motives (often accompanied by public acknowledgment) to respond to God's love for them. At Caesarea in Acts 10, we read of Cornelius, a centurion of the Italian regiment who is described as a God-fearing and generous person together with his whole family. The apostle Peter is led by God to speak to Cornelius. He and his family are led to receive the most generous gift of God, which is eternal life through Jesus Christ.

Generosity results in great joy, not only for those who benefit but also for those who give (Proverbs 11:25). As in the case of Cornelius, those who give open the door for greater spiritual riches for themselves and their families or communities. The community celebrates generous people (Proverbs 11:10). An example of this in the New Testament is Dorcas, who lives a life of generosity (Acts 9:36–41). When she dies there is great weeping as the widows, whom she helped with her sewing projects, plead with the apostle Peter to come to visit. In this case God raises her from the dead as a result of Peter's prayer.

Giving to the Poor

There are those who argue against giving to the poor, as this might create dependency, they argue, that it is not sustainable. Glenn Schwartz argues that all of us must depend on the Lord whether poor or rich. [25] Givers must trust God and respond to Him in their decisions, while those who receive must recognize and trust God as the provider. Our generosity must not create unhealthy dependence on the giver, whether we are giving time or money. Generosity should also not lead to "God complexes" that place those who give in a position of control over the recipients. Giving should always point people to the only One who sustains the universe (Hebrews 1:3).

John Rowell suggests that:

> Dependency need not be a problem, even when outside funding predominates, if Western contributions are made without strings being attached and if national leaders are able to assert themselves by taking their rightful role in casting vision and initiating ministry. If national leaders are truly autonomous and if they remain free from control exercised by more well-provisioned partners, the negative

---

25. Glenn J. Schwartz, *When Charity Destroys Dignity: Overcoming Unhealthy Dependency in the Christian Movement* (Lancaster, PA: World Mission Associates, 2007).

realities we associate with dependency can be largely reduced without denying legitimately needed support for the poor.[26]

Generosity is God's plan for sustainability. John Ashcroft argues that the primary economic unit is "the household, or three-generational family."[27] This recognizes that at least two generations in a family—children and the elderly—may not be productive. The productive generation must therefore work and meet the needs of those who are unable.

The apostle Paul writing to the Philippians (4:15) talks of "giving and receiving." When generosity is viewed as more than money, there is a healthy exchange of resources that includes prayer, time (giving ourselves), hospitality, material things such as food, and of course money. Rowell quotes Rickett when he speaks of fostering interdependency when Rowell says, "Unhealthy dependency occurs when reciprocity and responsibility are ignored, overvalued or undervalued."[28] The goal, he says, is to end outside dependency but not eliminate outside giving. Giving has always been God's way of sustaining His mission. We are members of one body, and we all need each other. One example of complementary giving is that of a mission trip undertaken by an African missionary to a very hostile environment. The high cost of the plane ticket to an otherwise inaccessible region was underwritten by a gift from a Western giver. The African missionary undertook this dangerous trip that almost cost his life when the light aircraft he flew with crash-landed. This was followed by a difficult period of illness. One can argue as to who gave the most—the one who gave the finances for the trip or the one who gave time and almost his life. It took both the gift of money and the time of the African to accomplish this task. Generosity is therefore both an opportunity for the givers and the receivers to experience wholeness. We need one another in the Body of Christ.

---

26. John Rowell, *To Give or Not to Give; Rethinking Dependency, Restoring Generosity, and Redefining Sustainability* (Tyrone, GA: Authentic Publishing, 2007).

27. John Ashcroft, *Jubilee Manifesto; A Framework, Agenda & Strategy for Christian Social Reform* (Leicester, England: Inter-Varsity Press, 2005).

28. Rowell, *To Give or Not to Give.*

Giving by the Poor

Generosity is not limited to those that have material resources. We observe that time and again, the poor too are required to give as part of their faith in God. Examples of this are the little boy and his fish (John 6:9) whose sacrifice leads to the feeding of five thousand and the poor widow who gives her last meal to the prophet Elijah and is sustained thereafter during three years of famine (1 Kings 17:8–16).

In Kenya one pastor of a church in a slum had only four members and an empty building. He chose to make the empty church building available for children in the community who could not afford to attend classes at school. He and the four church members chose to share not only their building but also their education skills. The parents of these children began to notice a positive change in their children, who had previously spent their days in the streets. This caused them to want to meet the pastor and become a part of his church. God has multiplied this act of generosity on the part of the pastor so that his act of love has now multiplied to impact over four hundred students per year who now attend church on Monday to go to school.

Living Generously Advances God's Justice

When Jesus begins his ministry in what has come to be known as the Nazareth Manifesto, he reads from the book of Isaiah:

> The Spirit of the Lord is on me, because he has anointed me to proclaim good news to the poor. He has sent me to proclaim freedom for the prisoners and recovery of sight for the blind, to set the oppressed free, to proclaim the year of the Lord's favor. (Luke 4:18–19)

Jesus speaks of a new dispensation of the Lord's favor—a time of jubilee. At Pentecost not only do we see a new community born but we also see a new social order, fulfilling the words of Jesus above. Kim Tan reminds us that this was the first time in the history of Israel that the Jubilee had ever been observed.

Tan describes what he calls the Jubilee programs that were established in the Old Testament:

- The tithing programs every three years (Deuteronomy 14:28; 26:12)
- The Sabbath programs every seven years (Deuteronomy 15; Leviticus 25)
- The Jubilee programs every fifty years [29]

The Jubilee had to do with how one related to capital, not just what they did with income. Most of our giving is tied to income. Jubilee relates to sustaining capital. The Jubilee programs described above had never been fulfilled. Those who have the economic power are not naturally inclined to cede this to others. At Pentecost the Spirit-filled Galileans could sell what they had and share with those in need.

This was not socialism, where people hold property in common—this was stewardship, where people continue to own and make personal choices as to what to do with what they own. When Ananias and Sapphira in Acts 5:1–5 try to benefit themselves and buy favor with their false generosity, judgment is swift. The early disciples were models of social justice, building the capacity of those who were marginalized.

Living Generously Needs to Be Intentional

There is need for one to have a clear life purpose that includes goals concerning how one desires to serve others. An understanding, development, and utilization of one's spiritual and natural talents builds a foundation for biblical stewardship.

Church leaders encourage people to give by encouraging them to tithe. Some will distinguish between tithes and offerings. Tithing is based on the Old Testament law. The tithe was first mentioned before the law of Moses was given. Abraham (Genesis 14:20) and Jacob (Genesis 28:20–22) both gave a tithe. Brian Anderson notes that both these men gave

---

29. Kim Tan, *The Jubilee Gospel: The Jubilee, Spirit and the Church* (Milton Keynes, UK: Authentic Media, Milton Keynes, 2008).

these tithes voluntarily.[30] But under the law, tithing became "mandatory upon all God's people." Anderson goes on to note that under the law, tithing was not in the form of money, but "the tithe is described as the product of the land, seed of the land, fruit of the tree, herd or flock." He concludes by noting that under the law, we see the tithe used in at least three ways.

In many respects, it appears that the tithe required under the law is similar to our governmental taxation today. Israel was ruled by a theocracy. Under that theocracy the people were responsible to support government workers (priests), holidays (festivals), and the poor (aliens, widows, and orphans).[31]

In the New Testament, tithing is not commanded. One is, however, encouraged to be intentional, joyful, and generous. Paul in 1 Corinthians 16:1–2 tells the Corinthians to plan their giving and be proportionate—giving in accordance with how much they get: "Now about the collection for the Lord's people: Do what I told the Galatian churches to do. On the first day of every week, each one of you should set aside a sum of money in keeping with your income, saving it up, so that when I come no collections will have to be made."

Anderson gives some biblical guidelines on giving, which can help us avoid the dangers of pride, power, and praise, discussed in Part I, or greed, passivity, and exploitation discussed in this chapter.[32] These are summarized below:

- We should give anonymously (Matthew 6:1–4).
- We should give voluntarily (2 Corinthians 8:3–4).
- We should give expectantly (2 Corinthians 9:6, 8–11; Proverbs 11:24–25, 19:17; Matthew 6:19–21; Luke 12:33; 1 Timothy 6:18–19).

---

30. Brian Anderson, "Old Testament Tithing vs. New Testament Giving," *Milpitas Bible Fellowship*, http://www.solidrock.net/library/anderson/sermons/ot.tithing.vs.nt.giving.php, accessed January 30, 2014.

31. Ibid.

32. Ibid.

- We should give cheerfully (2 Corinthians 9:7).
- We should give sacrificially (2 Corinthians 8:1–5; Mark 12:41–44).

I will add to this list and say one should give prayerfully in response to God first and not be driven by the multitude of needs around us. Those with material lack may be socially and spiritually wealthy (James 2:5). Those with material wealth may be socially and spiritually needy. Prayerful discernment allows us to joyfully contribute our gifts to the needy whether we or others are materially poor or rich, allowing us to reflect God's character of generosity and justice to a watching world.

Questions for Individual Reflection and Discussion in Small Groups

- How does your generosity reflect your love of and devotion to God? Are you happy with this reflection? If not, what one step will you take to have your generosity better reflect your love of and devotion to God?
- How does your generosity reflect the nature of your relationship with God? Are you happy with this reflection? If not, what one step will you take to have your generosity better reflect the depth of your relationship to God?
- How does your generosity promote biblical justice? If you cannot name a way, what step will you take for it to do so?
- Is your generosity intentional, and if so, what does that look like?

Christ-Centered Generosity
Becomes Visible in the Arab World

BY REV. MAHER FOUAD (MIDDLE EAST)

On a visit to the Syrian refugee camps in Lebanon, I met with some refugee ministers who had left their homes and properties in Syria and decided to commit all their time and efforts to serving the Syrian families there. I sat with some of them and their families, crowded into their one-room quarters with neither a kitchen nor a bathroom. I met with others who had no financial resources. At home they earned handsome incomes for their families, but the Lord called them to serve their fellow refugees. In all these situations, I witnessed how the Lord supplied for all of their financial resources—not only to cover their daily needs but also to cover all needs of the ministry they do.

In a village in Somalia, two Arab World Evangelical Ministers' Association (AWEMA) ministers were sent to plant churches. They lived in mud huts with no furniture. We learned, to our surprise, that they were building a very small church and had started to build a school. They had only the small salaries that AWEMA could send them. We discovered that they collected their tithes and added them to the tithes of other ministers living the same simple lives as theirs. Together, they aimed to have a place to invite people to worship God. The Lord rewarded their faithfulness by protecting them from the village people who worship other gods. The Lord also provided them with a church full of people who decided to leave their non-Christian backgrounds to live for Christ.

Thirty years ago AWEMA was just an idea. We had the dream of unifying efforts of the Arab Christian in twenty-two Arab countries to reach out to the Arab communities with the Gospel as well as supporting the under- and above-ground churches. We started by faith, and the Lord encouraged our simple faith with a large group of ministry partners from all over the world as well as with financial resources received from poor churches and personal donations from ministers who lived very simple lives in countries suffering extreme poverty. The real richness we received from the Lord throughout these thirty years has been the friendships and ministry partners who have spiritually and financially supported us. We learned to dream, pray, and expect the Lord to supply. The Lord has never forsaken us, not once! His presence was always real in everything we did, even in all the harsh circumstances of ministering in the Middle East.

The Old Woman and Her Tree

BY SAMUEL CHIANG (UNITED STATES AND HONG KONG)

S ome time ago, I was sitting on a little wooden stool at the back of an open church in China. The church had been built a few years back, and as I was sitting low on the wooden stool, there were some people standing at the windows outside, peering into the church as worship was due to commence.

One of the church leaders came to me and told me proudly who had donated the wooden stools. The name was lost on me. Then the same church leader insisted that I had been to her home, and I had to shuffle through my memory until finally I recalled this old woman. But how could this be? How did she manage to donate all the wooden stools? Where did she get the money?

Her home was a thatched-roof dwelling with two small rooms that provided a place for rest and a room to cook in, as well as entertain guests. I recalled walking into this house; her walls were caked with the residue of smoke and oil that had come from her cooking, and there was no electricity. And in her yard there was one single, large tree.

When the pastor of this open church had called for the congregants to give so that the new church could be built, this lady wanted to give. But she was poor, and she did not know how.

One day she came out of her home and looked around the yard. She saw that singular tree and wanted to donate it. Since she did not have a telephone in her place, she went next door and used the neighbor's landline to call the pastor's mobile phone. She told the pastor how she was going to donate to the church. The pastor said no, and they had an argument on the phone.

The old lady wanted to donate the only tree in her yard, but she was the only living person left in her clan. Some twenty years earlier, when her older relatives were dying and knew there would be no one to take care of her as she grew old, they planted a tree for her. In China, dying alone is a problem, as no one knows who will take care of you. The plan was that when this old woman died, her neighbor would come and cut down the tree, turn it horizontal, dig out the middle, place her body into it, and use it as a casket to bury her with dignity.

After arguing with the older woman, the pastor relented (as he would, because the younger person always respects the older). He and other members of the church came to cut down the tree and then carted it to the old church to put it on display so that all could see what this old woman had done.

The church rejoiced with her! They made wooden stools from that tree.

The plan was to cut down a living tree so as to put a dead body in it and bury it in the ground. Now, the plan changed so that a living tree was cut down and made into wooden stools. Then, the "spiritually dead" people who were outside of the church could sit on these dead wooden stools, and as they heard and received the Gospel, they could become "living" souls.

This old woman was shrewd in exchanging resources so as to welcome others into the Kingdom (Luke 16:9). When she died soon thereafter, did that local church take care of her? Absolutely!

What trees are standing around you that God is calling you to put to use for His work?

Generosity through the Eyes
of Two African Children

By Christie-Joy Offei Awuku and Eben-Joy Offei Awuku
(TWELVE AND TEN YEARS OLD, GHANA)

God made the beautiful sunshine, flowers, birds that sing, bright stars, beautiful mountains and seas, air we breathe, and plants that give us food. God made man and woman in His own image and likeness. All these are gifts of nature from a loving and generous God. God wants us to be like Him—this always makes Him very happy when we are. Generosity began with God who, at creation, gave a beautiful form and order to an empty and dark world.

In appreciation of all that God has given us—the sun, the moon and stars, the seas, all living things, our families, friends, and in fact our very lives—we as Christians must give our very lives to God and also give generously to God's people, God's work, and God's world! Giving to God can be in various forms. We can give our time, talents, and treasures to help others. We can help take care of the sick, refugees, orphans, the poor, and people with all sorts of needs. If Christ could offer his life for us, we must give cheerfully of the rich resources that God in His mercy has given us. Indeed, God blesses so that we can be a blessing to others.

We have been privileged to come across many generous people who spur us on to generosity. We would specifically like to mention our late headmistress, Mrs. Vincentia Woolhouse-Sackey, who died suddenly in 2014. Her short life was one of such cheerful sacrifice and generosity. She had an eye on each and every child in her care at school and even embraced our families too. She was a real mother to us. We recount how she showered our baby sister with beautiful and numerous gifts at her birth—nice clothing, toys, shoes, and even a baby walker too. Many other

Christian friends brought so many gifts for our kid sister that Daddy and Mummy did not have to shop for her till after her ninth month. Our family lost count of the gifts. Some gift items were dropped off without our knowledge of the givers.

Another show of generosity was with a Christian couple who adopted two orphan teenagers. Today the two children are in the university and doing well. These are acts that make Christians live as "the salt of the earth" and shine as "the light of the world" (Matthew 5:13–14).

We are learning from our parents and have decided to also live generous lives, often sharing our food and snacks with some needy friends and helping out as best as we can. For some years now, we have given out clothing, shoes, and several supplies from our home to orphans and needy children around us through a ministry called Touching Lives at Christmas. We make it a point to take good care of our books, clothes, shoes, and belongings because we always treasure the thought of passing them on in good shape to needy friends and others. Our family treasures joy as a practice of life. Our parents are teaching us to live as a joyful family by loving Jesus, loving ourselves at home, and loving others. We are learning to treat everyone God brings our way as special. It's not always easy, but it's always a great joy when we obey!

There is more blessing in giving than in receiving, especially when we give to people who don't have the means to return our favors. May Christ's work on the cross never be in vain as we also share our faith in loving God and loving our neighbors (Luke 10:27) by our kind acts of generosity! And what a beautiful world it would be if all the needs of our neighbors were met by our little efforts put together—adults and children alike. God is generous. Let us learn to glorify Him by our Christ-centered lives of generosity. Generosity is more than giving; it must be the lifestyle of the Christian and a golden mark of the church!

A Generosity Journey in South Korea

BY SUNG WOOK CHUNG (SOUTH KOREA)

My life is a product of God's generosity demonstrated by numerous people around me. I was born into a pastor's family. My father was a Presbyterian minister in South Korea. In the 1970s he was planting a church in the suburban area of Seoul when he inherited some money from his parents. Instead of spending it on himself, he used all of it for planting a church whose goal was to serve and encourage the poor in the name of Jesus Christ.

When I was seventeen years old, my father passed away after a long struggle with his health. My family was devastated by his sudden death. My mother was left alone and had to support herself and two sons financially. The first challenge that we had to overcome was the tuition for my high school education. By God's grace and my school's generosity, my tuition was waived and I was able to finish high school.

After graduating from high school, I faced the financial challenge of paying for my college education. Since my mother was serving a local church as an associate minister and her salary was not enough to support my college education, I had to depend on God's grace and people's generosity. Keimyung University awarded me a Bisa Special Scholarship, which covers full tuition for four years as well as a modest living stipend. Without this scholarship, I could not have graduated from the college.

Even more remarkably, I was able to finish my doctoral work at the University of Oxford with the help of a generous person. A cousin of my mother supported my study financially during my doctoral work from 1996 to 2000. Due to a serious financial crisis in South Korea in 1997,

83

I was struggling hard with financial difficulties. Her generosity helped me successfully finish my doctoral work.

On the basis of these personal stories, I am convinced that generosity is one of the greatest means for enhancing and extending the kingdom of God. As a beneficiary of numerous people's generosity, I now encourage people to be generous and to take every opportunity to be sacrificial in their giving.

As I encourage generosity, I still face frustrations and obstacles. So many Christians both in America and South Korea do not have proper understanding of biblical stewardship. They do not know why we should be generous and sacrificial givers. They have not been challenged to view Jesus Christ and his earthly ministry from the perspective of generosity. And they do not have a proper appreciation for the fact that the Triune God is the God of generous and sacrificial giving.

However, I have seen many Christians change their hearts and attitudes through my teaching and preaching ministry, which emphasizes the spiritual and theological significance of generous giving. Some of them have begun to contribute their money to the cause of saving lives of African children, and others have begun to donate to the cause of helping children suffering from tuberculosis.

What is your story of generosity? Can you map the places where the generosity of others has blessed you? How would God use you today to be that same blessing in the lives of others?

As a result of these beautiful stories, I have also changed. I have become more convinced that I should continue to teach fellow believers biblical stewardship and how to practice biblical principles of generosity in their everyday lives. I have also become a more generous person in giving and sharing my resources, time, energy, talents, and gifts. Praise the Lord!

PART IV

Christian Generosity in India

P. K. D. Lee (India)

Does India Have a Generous Culture?
Indian hospitality is well-known, and neighbors sharing and helping each other is a normal experience in Indian society. The borrowing of a cup of sugar or some other need in the kitchen is the norm rather than the exception. In many Indian cultures, the borrowed cup is not to be returned empty but must have something in it. These experiences and practices give an impression to the minds of most people that Indians are generous and the fabled Eastern hospitality is an essential part of Indian culture.

Yet three recent studies seem to contradict this understanding of Indian society. In the report titled *India Giving* the following statement is made:

> By any standard, these figures confirm that the amount of money given to formal charities in India is extremely small, no doubt under-lining the nascent nature of the charitable-giving environment in India and the need for charitable funds to come into India to support the social need there.[33]

Another study is in the report *Emerging Philanthropy Markets*.[34] The authors offer a graph indicating the propensity to support a given type of

---

33. Terrie Maple and Richard Harrison, *India Giving: Insights into the Nature of Giving Across India* (Delhi: Charities Aid Foundation, 2012), 32.

34. Richard Michon and Atul Tandon, "Emerging Philanthropy Markets," *International Journal of Nonprofit and Voluntary Sector Marketing* 17, no. 4 (2012): 352–62.

charity. In this ranking, India comes in near the bottom, ranking fiftieth out of sixty-one countries.

The third is the World Giving Index 2012[35], published by Charities Aid Foundation (CAF), which ranks countries for their generosity. Here India is ranked at 133 out of 146 countries. The study measures generosity in the categories of giving financial aid (India is 86 out of 146), giving time (106 out of 146), and helping strangers (146 out of 146).

These reports would indicate that while Indians give, they tend to give for religious reasons and to immediate neighbors but not to causes or charities. The CAF report also indicates that even though the majority of Indians give, the level of giving is low.

This does not mean that exceptions to the rule do not exist. Dave Toycen recounts a narrative Mother Teresa used to tell of a young Hindu couple who made a large donation to her.[36] When asked where they got the money from, they replied, "We got married two days ago. Before we got married we had decided not to celebrate the wedding, not buy wedding clothes, not to have a reception or a honeymoon. We wanted to give you the money saved."

Why did they do this? Their reply was "We love each other so much we wanted to share the joy of our love with those you serve."

This is a great example of generosity shown by an Indian Hindu couple because of the modeling of Christian generosity shown by Mother Teresa.

The Indian Mindset and Generosity

The concept of karma (fate) in India and much of Asia works against generosity. The theory of karma postulates that each of us earns a reward, either good or bad, because of our actions. So if someone is suffering, it is because of his bad karma earned and there is little I can do about it. However, if I give a small help, I earn good karma. Because of this, charity

---

35. "World Giving Index 2012," Charities Aid Foundation, 2012, 66, https://www.cafonline .org/publications/2012-publications/world-giving-index-2012.aspx.

36. Dave Toycen, *The Power of Generosity: How to Transform Yourself and Your World* (Toronto: HarperCollins, 2004), 59.

motivated by love was not the norm in Indian behavior before the impact of Christian influence and education. Christ-centered generosity is not the mindset of the normal Indian Christian. Average Indians will give their neighbors small amounts of help to earn good karma, but sacrificial giving does not exist.

Most giving in India is motivated by pity rather than by compassion. Sacrificial giving comes from compassion that flows out of our love for Christ. In contrast, giving out of pity has two motivations—feeling that the other person is weak and inferior or from the desire to earn merit through giving. Toycen references Paul Baetz, who was crippled, with:

> Reflecting on his own situation, Paul described to me the distinction between pity and compassion. People who pity him are a dime a dozen, he says, but those who have compassion are fewer. In his words, compassion is a desire for relationship with the one who is suffering; pity is merely a feeling that in many cases avoids relationship.[37]

God in His generosity gave His son for us that He could have a relationship with us. That is the greatest example of generosity, which we are called to model in our life. This is the generosity of the gospel. However, the missionaries who came to India did not teach this kind of Christ-centered generosity.

When the missionaries came to India, they did not understand the Indian mindset. Seeing the poverty Indians lived in, the missionaries began giving to them rather than teaching them sacrificial giving and financial responsibility. Because of this behavior of the missionaries and the norm of society around them, the Indian church was not taught or equipped to give sacrificially.

There were notable exceptions. Some in Indian leadership, like Bishop V. S. Azariah and Pandita Ramabai, began to teach the people of the need to give sacrificially and to be self-sufficient. But while they had some

---

37. Ibid., 33.

influence, by and large the church in India tended to become dependent on the West. The great generosity of the Western church did not help the Indian church in learning the importance of generosity.

Because of the lack of apparent connection between the gospel and generosity as such, generosity was never emphasized in the teaching of the church. People were encouraged to invite Jesus into their lives and to preach the gospel. However, being generous was never an expected response, and the connection between the gospel and generosity was never established.

I accepted Jesus fairly late in life, at the age of twenty-nine. Having grown up in a family that was miserly to an extreme and had no generosity of any kind, I never took the practice of generosity seriously. I left generosity to my wife, who grew up in a generous household. For me spiritual growth took the form of legalism.

The Problem of Legalism

In Part I of this book, Scott Rodin points out the difference between philanthropy and Christ-centered generosity. His main emphasis is that the motivations are different though the acts may appear to be the same. The Christian motivation comes from recognizing God as the owner of all things and our role as faithful and joyful stewards. As stewards we reflect the heart of God in the way we steward the good things God entrusted to us. We have shown how Indian giving falls short of this understanding of the faithful steward.

Part of the challenge of legalism has to do with the Hindu mindset, which is strongly work oriented. You do work to earn good karma, or rewards. The other teaching in Hinduism is dharma, or duty. One must do one's duty at whatever cost.

This forms a very legalistic mindset, where a man will carry out his work not because of a belief in its merits per se, or in its necessity, but solely because it is his duty to do so. The motivation is either the earning of merit or the carrying out of an obligation. The motivation is not love or gratitude.

This has continued into the church as well. Here the Old Testament commands to obey the law tend to outstrip the motivation of love that results in Christ-centered generosity. Our life becomes a reflection of the law rather than of the love of Christ. When the law rules, the burden for the lost is replaced by the command to "go," and righteousness is seen as coming from the obedience to the law rather than from the love for God and humankind.

In his analysis of generosity, Rodin has said that the motives can be either material reward or praise, neither of which leads to Christ-centered generosity. These alternative motives militate against Christ-centered generosity and make us no different from the non-Christian world around us.

Another factor affecting Asian thinking is that society tends to be strongly vertical, where the authority of the elders is not challenged and is obeyed without question. As a result, the Asian church tends to be submissive and compliant toward its leaders, never questioning the motives behind their actions. Because of this, church members do not usually examine their own inner motivations for their actions, but rather they look to their elders for guidance. This tends to make them lean toward legalism rather than love and faithfulness as the basis for their actions.

Generosity Redefined

In this discussion we need to widen the meaning of the term "generosity." The definition that the National Generosity Network in India gives is "a response of love in recognizing God's ownership of all things, and his grace to us in giving salvation and blessings, and this generosity leads to a positive view of people and situations resulting in putting others before self and a sharing of time, money and resources." [38]

Koshy Verghese, one of the prominent Christian business executives and church leaders involved with the generosity movement in India, gave this definition in his speech on his seventieth birthday celebration: "Generosity is any thought, word or deed that brings hope, love, peace

---

38. "Need for the Conference," National Generosity Network, 2013, http://www.generos itynetwork.in/conference.

and/or joy to someone else." Generosity is not only about money but also about how we look on and interact with others.

Lack of generosity in these terms seems to be the norm in India. We see it in the driving habits of Indians, in their behavior in queues, and in their impatience in crowds. Unfortunately, these behaviors tend to be found in the Indian church as well. When these public behaviors are compared with the same behavior in countries that have been Protestant for generations and a Christian ethos has permeated into their culture, we can see a remarkable difference.

At a presentation I gave on the lack of generosity in India because of Hinduism at a seminary last year, some in attendance argued that India is not really Hindu. The argument was that the Hindus were the oppressors, which included all and sundry as Hindus, even though they were not Hindus but rather animists, and it would be incorrect to apply Hindu thinking to most of India. While the neo-Buddhist and Christians might rightly argue that much of the population were outcasts from Hinduism and so not Hindus per se, the fact is that living in the midst of a large, uniform, Hindu society, all have been influenced by this thinking and behavior to some extent, including Christians.

When I accepted Christ, I was thrown into a group of hyperactive believers who were totally committed to serving Christ. But the general tenor of our behavior was arrogant and condemnatory of others. The group would encourage us not to be involved in the church, as they were unspiritual and we were spiritual. The motivation for our actions was obedience to Christ rather than love for Christ and for people. When I look back to our behavior now, I am appalled by the lack of Christian generosity we showed. But we were not the exception; this seemed to have been the norm in evangelical circles.

There was no sense of the enormity of the grace of God that would automatically lead to forgiving and accepting others. There was no sense of what Rodin has said of partnering in the generosity of Jesus. Jesus taught that if we were aware of the forgiveness of God in our life, the love of God would express itself through our life and we would forgive others. So if that generosity and love is absent from our life, it means that we have not tasted the forgiveness of Jesus and so may not have salvation. But when we have experienced the forgiveness of God in our life, we have no problem in forgiving others and being generous in our outlook. I know many Christians who profess to be sincere in their faith but are unable to forgive people with whom they have had differences of opinion. They do a lot of work for the Kingdom, but their motivations are duty and the command to "go," not a passion and love for people.

It was C. B. Samuel, when he was the director of the Evangelical Fellowship of India Commission on Relief (EFICOR), who challenged my thinking by asking me to explain Matthew 11:1–6. We see Jesus's response to the disciples of John the Baptist in Matthew 11:4–6 as follows:

> Jesus answered and said unto them, Go and show John again those things which ye do hear and see: The blind receive their sight, and the lame walk, the lepers are cleansed, and the deaf hear, the dead are raised up, and the poor have the gospel preached to them. And blessed is he, whosoever shall not be offended in me.

Here all the people received physical healing, except for the poor who had the gospel preached to them. Obviously in the context, the gospel here was a physical solution to the needs of the poor. How does this happen? I believe it happens by the transformation of the hearts of the rich so that they are willing to share their wealth with the poor in the Kingdom. Thus, in the kingdom of God, the poor experience not only physical deliverance from poverty but also from injustice, rejection, and dehumanization. This is the essence of the gospel.

Sandhya joined my office as an executive assistant and later became the head of one of the departments. Her nature is to be generous, not only with money but also with time, love, and concern. Soon she became the adopted mother for all in the office, and slowly the office culture changed. Our work environment became a place where people's needs were met, and people looked after and cared for each other. All visitors made mention that the atmosphere in the office was amazing, and they envied us. Though the office closed in 2007, Sandhya is still in contact with the staff and continues to be a blessing to them. When the office closed, the staff kept coming in to the office, though there was no work or pay, because it had become their family and home. This is the Christ-centered generosity of the kingdom of God.

Cause for Alarm in the Church

In Matthew 6:23 Jesus says a phrase used in only one other place in the New Testament. The phrase is "if your eye be evil." Jesus says, "But if your eye be evil, thy whole body shall be full of darkness. If therefore the light that is in you be darkness, how great is that darkness!" What does it mean? It is important to understand the phrase if our life is not to be full of darkness.

In Matthew 20:15, Jesus asks the laborers who are offended at all the workers being paid the same amount irrespective of how many hours they had worked, "Is it not lawful for me to do what I will with mine own? Is your eye evil, because I am good?" Here, the eye being evil means lacking generosity and being critical.

So in Matthew 6:23, Jesus is saying that if we lack generosity and are critical in the way we look at people and situations, our life is full of darkness. Generosity is the light that makes our life bright.

If this is so, then lack of generosity seriously harms the church, as it makes the church full of darkness, and the light in the church fails to be a witness to the nations.

When we consider the number of Jesus's parables and teachings that are about money and generosity, the lack of generosity in the church is clearly a cause for concern. In the parable of the unforgiving servant in Matthew 18:23–35, Jesus clearly teaches that when we have been forgiven our sins, we need to be forgiving toward others. The servant who was unforgiving was handed over to his tormentors until his debts were paid. His debt or sin came back on him, and his salvation was lost.

We see a similar teaching in the Lord's Prayer, where Jesus says that if we do not forgive others then God would not forgive us, indicating that we would not have salvation. The teaching would appear to be that once we have experienced the forgiveness of Jesus Christ in our life, we would be so flooded with gratitude and the sense of the enormity of the grace of God that we would automatically forgive others, and the love of God would express itself through our life. So, if that generosity and love is absent from our life, it means that we have not fully tasted the forgiveness of Jesus. As Rodin said, we partake and share in the generosity of Jesus, and that is our lifestyle. When that happens, there is no hesitance in our desire to forgive others.

In John 13:35 Jesus says, "By this shall all men know that ye are my disciples, if ye have love one to another."

Our witness is the love and fellowship within the community of the Kingdom. The physical manifestation of this community is the church. If this love is not manifested, our witness dies. If there is one family going to bed hungry in your church, the fullness of the gospel does not exist.

If this is so, the absence of Christ-centered generosity in the church harms its witness and may be one of the reasons for the slow statistical growth of the church in India.

It used to be that when I went out into the world, especially when I was shopping or dealing with somebody who was selling me a product, I tended not to be generous. I found that this was because I was expecting to be served and was not going out with the attitude of serving others. Because of this I could be (and often still am) highly critical and often upset at the service. This left me without a witness and no opportunity to share the gospel with the people with whom I dealt.

When analyzing my behavior, I found that the root cause was my attitude of wanting to be served instead of wanting to serve. As Christians we need to step out in Christ's love with the intention of being a blessing in someone's day rather than looking for others to meet our needs first. That is Christ-centered generosity, and it is through Christ-centered generosity that we can be witnesses to the abundant generosity of God toward us.

Raja did not have much education, and so he did not have many financial resources. But one day he was touched in his heart when he saw a destitute man lying on a rubbish heap. Moved by his compassion, he put the man in an auto rickshaw and took him home so that he could provide comfort for him. Slowly, he began bringing more and more people to his home from the roadside. This act of unconditional love has now become a ministry involving his whole family, as they live with the destitute and share with them the same food they eat. That is Christ-centered generosity that bears witness to the word of God's transforming grace in us.

Responsible Generosity in an Age of Dependence

In the early church, generosity was the hallmark of the Body of Christ. We see it being practiced in Acts 2:42–47 and 4:32–37. However, this generosity led to much misuse, as parasites began to live off the church instead of working. We see signs of this in the epistles. In I Timothy 5:16, Paul directs members of the church look after their own families and not pass on the responsibility to the church. Similarly, in 2 Thessalonians 3:10, Paul commands that people need to work and feed themselves, and if they do not work, they will not be given food.

In Didache chapter 1, it says:

> Happy is he who gives according to the commandment, for he is guiltless. Woe to him who receives; for if one receives who has need, he is guiltless; but he who receives not having need shall pay the penalty, why he received and for what. And coming into confinement, he shall be examined concerning the things which he has done, and he shall not escape from there until he pays back the last penny. And also concerning this, it has been said, Let your alms sweat in your hands, until you know to whom you should give. [39]

---

39. "The Didache," Early Christian Writings, Roberts-Donaldson English Translation, accessed December 22, 2014, http://www.earlychristianwritings.com/text/didache-roberts.html.

This is a warning to those who live off the church. Generosity can breed a lack of generosity in some weak people. This can cause those who should be generous to be wary and, in the process, back away from their generosity.

This tendency to create dependency through our generosity does a lot of harm to the church, and so we are caught in a vicious cycle of generosity breeding dependence. The solution is not a lack of generosity or too much caution, but it is responsible generosity. This means that we need to teach the importance of giving so that the weak realize that they are harming themselves spiritually by trying to live off the church.

Another major hurdle faced in India is the accusation by the Hindu fundamentalists and also the government that we are being generous to win people to Christ, that it is not a natural generosity arising out of love. And so acts of generosity are looked at with suspicious eyes, especially when evangelism takes place at the same time.

We need to be careful that generosity is truly the natural expression of our love and not a strategy for evangelism. Unfortunately, some mission bodies have not only made it a strategy for evangelism but have also said so in their written documentation. This creates problems for the government with these bodies. While our generosity should not be dependent on the perception of the fundamentalist Hindus or the Indian government, it should be the expression of our faith and a core component to our discipleship and lifestyle. Simply put, we cannot be Christians and not be generous.

A Three-Pronged Strategy

We have shown that Christ-centered generosity is not normal in the Indian context. This situation acts like a two-edged sword for the church. On the one hand, this is an area where the church can make a tremendous impact in showing the difference Jesus makes to people and to society. On the other hand, it is difficult for the members of the Indian church—because of the influence of the society they live in and because of their own immersion in Hindu thinking—to make the radical transformation Jesus calls on Indians to make. Leading people to express belief in Jesus is easier than forming a community that lives by the principles of the Kingdom, as seen in the Sermon on the Mount, or the picture of the kingdom of God, as seen in the Old Testament prophecies like Isaiah 9:7. We need to ensure that we lay the foundation of the kingdom of God and not just an individualistic salvation for the maximum impact on the people of India with the gospel.

Hence, generosity needs to be taught as a part of the process of making disciples. This is extremely important to the Indian church, as this is where we can show our difference to Indians. Without this, the church has failed to grow and have the impact God desires. For this to be accomplished, all the churches need to engage in this movement. This will require a multipronged strategy to reach the message across the churches in India. Here is what I propose.

The first prong would be to impress on the church leadership the importance and urgency of the message of generosity going out to their members for their own spiritual nurture and the witness of the church. To achieve this we would have to take the help of Bible Schools and denominational leaders to teach the clergy the theological and practical connection between the gospel and generosity as a required response of our faith in Jesus as brought out by James and Jesus. To reach the head of denominations and Bible Schools, we would have to organize conferences for this group of people through platforms that bring them together, like the National Council of Churches in India, Evangelical Fellowship of India, etc.

The second prong is to reach the laity through a movement of teaching generosity through conferences and programs open to members of all churches in India. If enough of the laity in a church is impacted, these people will bring pressure on the church leadership to take the movement seriously and see that the church takes up the agenda of generosity.

The third prong would be to reach our mission organizations so that they would include the aspect of generosity as a part of the gospel and their teaching to new believers. The missionaries need to remember that the Christian life is an outcome of the love of God and the empowerment of the Holy Spirit, not a fear of the law or its demands.

I believe that this three-pronged approach can bring a change in the Indian church that would make it a vibrant witness to the transformative power of the gospel in Indian society.

Conclusion

Toycen quotes Samuel Oliner, who was rescued from the Holocaust with help from a peasant Christian family.[40] Later he researched some fifty thousand cases of non-Jews helping the Jews during the Holocaust. He found that education and religion were not determinant factors in making people generous. Instead, he found that the rescuers had learned generosity from at least one of their parents, who modeled generous and caring behavior for someone beyond their local group or clan.

This means that unless the church models generosity, its congregation cannot learn generosity. This puts a responsibility on the pastors to teach and encourage their pastorate committees to be generous and make the church into an epitome of generosity.

As Toycen says, "Who are the generous? They are ordinary people who are driven by an extraordinary desire and attitude to help others. They can be children, teenagers, adults, and senior citizens."[41]

It would be an error to think that the message of generosity is to be addressed to the rich. It needs to be addressed to the whole church—the young, the old, the poor, and the rich.

Questions for Individual Reflection and Discussion in Small Groups

- Why do you believe churches tend not to link the gospel with generosity? Does your church? Why or why not?
- Is your generosity motivated by obligation or by a love for Christ and neighbor? What has shaped that view?
- How does your church model generosity? How do you model generosity to your family, your community, and the world?

---

40. Toycen, *Power of Generosity*, 20–21.

41. Ibid., 27.

The Ukraine Responds with Joy

PROVIDED BY BARBARA SHANTZ (CANADA)

The following stories are excerpts from the Trans World Radio publication *Speaking Hope Through Giving Hearts*, which is available on the TWR Faith Reliance website: www.twr.org/faith-reliance. They are a small sample of the letters that TWR has received from our listeners in the Ukraine. We are touched by the hearts of generosity coming from such a troubled place in our world.

Mrs. R. Y., from Dnepropetrovsk province, Ukraine:

Dear servants in God's vineyard! I am in church once a month. My health does not allow me to go more often. I go only when I receive my pension so that I can bring to church my tithe. I live alone. I have nobody, except my Savior. I am 85 years old. And I guess I could say that I am not needed. But I find myself being a minister for the Lord because "faith without works is dead."

I have eight places to which I send donations. Just like today, when I received my pension, I immediately made distributions to each of these places. The first priority was the prison ministry, then the rest followed. And again it happened that I had nothing left for TWR. Then I remembered that I had a viburnum shrub, which I had already taken many times to the market, but nobody even took an interest. (The market is very close to me—about two minutes' walk).

And so I prayed to the Lord: "Dear Lord! For a second time already, I received a letter from TWR, and I have no money to give to your servants. Please, could you make it so that when I take the branches of this shrub to the market, all of it will be bought by one person. Then I will know that I have to send this money to TWR."

And so I went with my small cart full of viburnum to the market, and I had not yet spread it out when a woman came by and said, "I am taking all of it." And she bought all of it! After this I went straight to the post office and sent you the money for TWR. That is how the Lord gave you 50 hryvnia [about $6 USD].

Mrs. R. N., from Odessa province, Ukraine:

I am so grateful to you. I saw you all in the picture. It is so touching. You are bringing the Word of God to us. I was so happy to receive an answer to my problem. I gave the postman 1,000 hryvnia [about $117 USD] to send to you and bring me the receipt for it. Having done that made me want to jump for joy. I do trust that in a few months I will be able to send you something again. I am in debt before God. I am listening to His Word every day!

Mr. & Mrs. K., from Odessa province, Ukraine:

Dear staff of TWR. Thank you so much for your ministry of spreading the Gospel over the radio and for the spiritual food you are preparing for us. In our village there is a small church—a total of nine members. Yet the ladies listening to your programs would like to honor God with what they have—prayer and financial help. Thus, listening to the program about orphans, they have asked us to send you the included 1,000 hryvnia [about $117 USD] to pass on to these orphans.

Freedom to Live the Generous Life
as God's Stewards

BY PATRICK KUWANA (ZIMBABWE)

Understanding God's economic framework is pivotal to living the life of freedom as we generously bless the world with God's abundance. The very first words that God spoke over mankind set the foundation for this understanding. Genesis 1:28 says, "God blessed them and said to them, "Be fruitful and increase in number; fill the earth and subdue it. Rule over the fish in the sea and the birds in the sky and over every living creature that moves on the ground." It is critical for us to understand that God created a world with vast resources and not scarcity and that he intended for us to be stewards and not owners. Without this foundational understanding, it becomes very difficult for us to live a life of freedom that is overflowing with generosity because our worldview and hence behavior will be based on scarcity.

I believe the greatest lie that the devil has managed to get mankind to believe is that we live in a world that has scarce resources. It is this lie that has been ingrained into the world economic system that is based on the "ownership of scarce resources" and has resulted in manmade scarcity because of greed, materialism, and ultimately the worship of money as the center of security (instead of God). Interestingly, it's exactly what Jesus warned against when he said, "No one can serve two masters. Either you will hate one and love the other, or you will be devoted to one and despise the other. You cannot serve both God and money" (Matthew 6:24).

The very worldview of scarcity is one that questions the goodness of God. How can a loving Father create children and place them in an earth that does not have enough resources for them to survive?

The poverty spirit that we see in avenging people and nations comes out of this belief that God created a world with scarcity. This spirit stops those with more than enough from sharing with those without because it makes them fearful for their security and provision into the future and hence keeps them bonded in captivity to Mammon.

God has created us in His image and given us dominion to steward His earth, and as we do that, we are to use the vast resources He has given us in service to Him and to man. God has created an earth with abundance and not scarcity. God has called us to no longer live for ourselves but for Christ to fulfill the ministry of reconciling the world to Him (2 Corinthians 5:14–20). These vast resources that He has made available on the earth are to be used to fulfill this mandate.

We never have to be fearful of provision if we understand and live under His economic framework. God set up this framework so that every believer can live in freedom as a generous steward so that we can fulfill the Abrahamic covenant of being a blessing to all the families and nations of the world.

The Power of Christ-Centered Generosity and Prayer

By Liz Adleta (United States)

Twenty years ago, my husband, our eight children, and I were living in a village hoping to see God's kingdom coming more and more among the unreached people groups living in a neighboring nation as well as around us. There were already a few other folks from outside the area living there with their hearts longing for the same thing. As we prayed and worked together, we discovered thirty or so fellowships of various denominations existed in the community. But sadly, most were not connecting with one another in ministering to the community. Furthermore, there were some deep-seated offenses that divided the leaders and generated rumor, gossip, and bad blood in general. This condition drove us to prayer, crying out to God to reconcile the differences and heal the wounds of the past so that the Body of Christ could function as He intended.

As we prayed, God inspired an idea that we, the outsiders, host a pastors' breakfast for all the leaders in the village in honor of their service to the Lord in such a difficult area. For us, it was a sacrifice to the Lord, a seed we could sow for the sake of His kingdom. We issued printed invitations to each leader personally as we reserved a beautiful venue and made all the arrangements. As we prayed, we felt God leading us to ask six particular pastors from different denominations to lead in prayer at the event. We continued to pray as the time drew near for the event, believing God would do what only He could do to resolve those differences.

The day arrived, and most of those invited attended, drawn by the promise of good food and a lovely venue perhaps as much as anything else. We began by having each of us as the outsiders and hosts share briefly about how much we felt God was delighted by the service of those gathered, giving honor to whom honor was due as He directed. Then we asked the first pastor to lead out in prayer, never imagining what might happen next.

As the pastor began to pray, a strong sense of God's presence came among us, and the pastor began to weep. He began to confess to God in prayer as the Holy Spirit was convicting him, asking forgiveness of the other brothers and sisters. All of us were also being moved to tears as we listened. The gentle movement of the Spirit continued as one after the other of the pastors met together with all of us at the foot of the cross before His presence. God had birthed a sense of generosity in our hearts toward the leaders in the area. Now, watered by our prayers, that generosity was bearing fruit in the lives of these who had labored long and been wounded over the course of time. God was releasing healing and restoring relationships in an amazing way. We were told later that most of those continued meeting monthly to carry on working shoulder to shoulder for His glory.

Whatever our hands find to do, we should be doing it with our might for His glory. Our passionate love of Father, of Jesus, and of His Spirit naturally overflows to those around us. His love flows to us, through us, and out to all those around us just as a spring of water bubbles up and flows outward. We can then say, "We delight to do your will, Father." As we draw near to Him, we catch His heart of love for those around us. It becomes a delight to share the bountiful gifts He gives us with others as a natural result of His generosity to us. With the same measure we use, He measures again to us. It becomes an unending circle of delight, thankfully receiving His bounty to us, delighting to share with others of that bounty, and being even filled again from His unlimited heavenly storehouses. As Jesus did, we are doing what we see the Father doing. Let us then not only abide in His amazing presence but also actively choose to reflect His generous nature to the watching world. For the joy set before us.

Generosity and the Healing of the Land

BY GRAHAM POWER (SOUTH AFRICA)

My childhood years are filled with stories of a family that lived from month to month. Despite our financial situation, there was a great wealth of love and joy. Without my realizing it, generosity was a living reality in my family. My siblings left school early so that I could complete my schooling, an act that required generosity of time and a desire to share learning with the entire family. These actions of generosity became ingrained in my mind and would later become the blueprint for understanding that God often requires us to make personal sacrifices as we live a life of generosity and obedience.

After years of working hard and becoming a successful businessman with access to great amounts of wealth and a comfortable lifestyle, I met Christ and He turned my life upside down. My perspective of wealth and generosity changed as I began to acknowledge that success and wealth were from God, who had given me the gifts of entrepreneurship and business. He had provided the opportunities for me to gather wealth. Now, as His child, I became determined to be a conduit that God could use to redistribute the wealth that He had given me.

It's as we see in Deuteronomy 8:17–18: "You may say to yourself, 'My power and the strength of my hands have produced this wealth for me.' But remember the Lord your God, for it is he who gives you the ability to produce wealth, and so confirms his covenant, which he swore to your forefathers, as it is today."

Living in South Africa, we are faced with a daily reality of the inequality between the rich and the poor. Knowing that God had blessed me to be a blessing to others, I searched the Scriptures for guidance on how to use and distribute my wealth. While studying I also discovered that there are various forms of poverty—financial and relational poverty are both realities. Many people focus on the alleviation of financial poverty, but I knew that God was calling me to also cross racial, spiritual, and financial borders and to meet people at their point of need. It interested me to discover that the financially rich are often relationally poor, while the physically poor are often relationally rich. This reality is evident as we see so many wealthy people who question their friends and continually search for meaning and significance.

As my commitment to Christ deepened, God continued to show me that generosity is not a public giving that draws the attention of others but is instead an act of obedience and that He loves a cheerful giver. This revelation resulted in the formation of a trust foundation for the Power Group of Companies. A percentage of our profits is given to the needy of our community, including the poor, orphans, and disadvantaged South African youth. While this trust fund receives many applications for assistance, I have asked God to direct me to several NGOs and ministries that are working at a grassroots level with the people of South Africa, and we have focused our attention on assisting them. This allows us to contribute to the development of several ministries rather than just giving at random to a broad-based support group.

God has blessed me with a family that is also increasingly becoming aware of God's abundance to us. Together we have formed a family foundation. This fund is financed from personal giving, and together we have discovered that no matter the global economic situation, we cannot out-give God. God gives so that we can empty our hands, and when they are empty, He can refill them again, but I believe it depends on our attitude. We are grateful to God for what He has provided.

As we see in Proverbs 3:9–10: "Honor the Lord with your wealth, with the firstfruits of all your crops; then your barns will be filled to overflowing, and your vats will brim over with new wine."

In 2001 we hosted the first Day of Prayer for the city of Cape Town. It was a gathering of forty-five thousand Christians who not only prayed for our city and nation but also repented over the injustices of our past. Over the next two years, God showed us that praying is the first step in the transformation process but that we need to move to the practical application of God's love for the city. Our actions are the direct expression of God's love to a city that is surrounded by poverty. We then included the Days of Giving. This was an opportunity for the city to gather and share with those who were less fortunate. People all around the city responded, and within days we had warehouses filled with clothing, furniture, school uniforms, and even vehicles. All donations were distributed through local churches, and as reports filtered back about the gratitude and joy of those who received, we realized that God was calling His church to a lifestyle of generosity.

I acknowledge that single acts of generosity are not enough to alleviate the great needs we have in our nation, but I do believe that if every child of God would trust Him with their finances, we have the potential to change the face of our city and even our nation. As we give to God, we perform acts of service that, according to 2 Corinthians 9:12, lead to expressions of thanksgiving.

If we could learn to give and share what God has so freely given us, more parents would see their children go to bed with at least one meal a day, educational standards would improve, crime and theft would diminish, and together we could bring about God's kingdom on earth. This is a vision that I long to see fulfilled not only in my city but also around the world. We have enough resources to make this vision a reality, but we all just need to learn more from a God who was so generous that He gave us His best—His son.

2 Chronicles 7:14 has become a key challenge and promise that I wear on my arm (via an armband). I believe this is a key challenge that we pray—"turn from our wicked ways"—and then we will see the Lord's promise—"then will I hear from heaven, and I will forgive their sin and heal their land."

May God forgive our sins and heal our land.

PART V

Generosity: Latin American Perspective

By Rev. Edison Queiroz (Brazil)

Ll Christians on our planet need to know the principles of Christ-centered generosity. We live in a world full of selfishness, and for the Christian, it is a great challenge to live generously.

Looking at the Latin American continent, we face the same paradox as that of other continents. Namely, poverty leads people to be more caring and generous, while economic growth brings with it a strong appeal to the desire to own and accumulate property and wealth. As the opportunity for economic development grows across our continent, there is a corresponding need to learn, understand, and apply the concepts of Christ-centered generosity.

The Politics of Generosity in Latin America

Christianity in Latin America is only five hundred years old. Christopher Columbus, along with other explorers, reached its shores in the late 1400s and began the colonization process. This was done with much bloodshed and the sacrifice of thousands of Indians. Among the colonizers were people of bad character. In Brazil, for example, the Portuguese colonizers brought people who were known as "Degraded." These were convicted prisoners who would be in charge of taking care of the new world. In order to start exploring the continent, the colonizers used the native Indian tribes as slaves and also brought many people from Africa for the same purpose. The result was a strong racial mixture and a culture lacking essential life values, leaving scars that are evident in many areas of society today.

On the issue of stewardship, this inherited culture produced certain milestones that guided attitudes. The concept of ownership became very strong, and many people began using shady means to achieve their financial goals. Bribery and corruption became rampant, accepted in society as the means to achieve and hold positions of power and leadership. For example, the Brazilian people were spreading the concept of "taking advantage in everything," no matter the means. Another attitude was "find a way," which carried the idea that the ends justify the means.

The political instability in some Latin American countries also highlighted the fragility of the world system, showing that what we think we have is in reality based on a very fragile system. Each totalitarian government determines for itself to whom things will belong.

I was once preaching the gospel and bringing some aid to Christians and churches in Cuba. When I arrived there, a pastor met me at the airport. When I entered his car, he curiously started asking me questions about cars. He told me that the car we were riding in had a Skoda body, a Ford engine, a Chevrolet gearbox, and the list went on. I was amazed with the creativity, adaptability, and determination of the Cuban people in surviving in the midst of great needs. I asked that pastor, "Is this automobile yours?" He replied, "Here in Cuba, nobody owns anything because everything belongs to the government Communist Party. For now I'm using it, but any time the government can take away." Situations like this make it clear that the system of control over goods and riches is fragile and unstable.

On the other hand, the capitalist influence has created in people the idea that they need to have a lot of possessions in order to face the future. This has led some people to become slaves of compulsiveness in purchases. They purchase things they don't need only to fulfill the pleasure of buying and owning.

Unfortunately, some segments of Christianity have also been strongly influenced by this same mentality. While teaching on stewardship in our churches has been fueled by a strong emphasis on tithing and offering, we as Christians must understand more deeply the concept that everything comes from Him and belongs to Him, and we must obey His directions with joy.

Three Challenges We Face

We face three challenges in helping Christians turn back to the word of God, learn, and live the biblical principles of Christ-centered generosity.

The Challenge of Humanism

Many churchgoing people in Latin America have been influenced by the humanistic idea that human beings are the center of everything. This concept is very dangerous because it seeps its way subtly into our churches and even claims to have theological support.

This form of humanism teaches that Jesus died to make us good people and improve our lives. It believes that the whole creation was made for our own benefit, the angels exist to serve us, and God is the supplier of all our wants and needs. In other words, everything is about us and God exists for our benefit.

Some messages preached in churches and in the media proclaim that God is powerful and His power is intended only to help humankind reach their own goal—namely, being free from evil and attaining happiness. These preachers are losing the heart of the Gospel, where everything is about God and His Glory and not about the fulfillment of human desires.

The Bible says that God is the center of all things and that He alone is worthy of glory. Everything He does in our life is for His own glory.

Of course the Bible tells us that God wants to bless the people He created, but the ultimate goal is not to feed humanity's selfish desires. Everything the human being does must be for God's glory and not for personal satisfaction. The apostle Paul made this clear when he said, "So whether you eat or drink or whatever you do, do it all for the glory of God" (1 Corinthians 10:31).

We must face this insipid humanism that links itself to the natural tendencies to own and consume. We must confront it with a clear statement of Christ-centered generosity based on a theology of the faithful steward and the joy of selfless living.

The Challenge of the Prosperity Theology

There are also strong influences of the theology of prosperity in some of the church movements of Latin America, which teaches that following Jesus is the same as entering into a life of financial success, social projection, and immunity to any kind of suffering.

This theology openly teaches that poverty is evil and that God wants His children to be wealthy and own many things. Instead of promoting biblical stewardship, it promotes the concept that it is God's will for us to desire possessions and that true happiness consists in having them. Supporters forget these powerful words of Jesus: "Then he said to them, 'Watch out! Be on your guard against all kinds of greed; life does not consist in an abundance of possessions'" (Luke 12:15). We must face this challenge with the following biblical concepts.

We Are Only Passing Through This World

> *Dear friends, I urge you, as foreigners and exiles, to abstain from sinful desires, which wage war against your soul. —1 Peter 2:11*

The Bible is very clear about the limitations of time we have here on this planet. We are *pilgrims*, a word that in the original language gives the idea of someone living in a place with no right of citizenship. We are outsiders, which indicates that we are passing through here and our true home is in heaven.

We Shall Not Take Anything from Here to Heaven

> *For we brought nothing into the world, and we can take nothing out of it. But if we have food and clothing, we will be content with that. Those who want to get rich fall into temptation and a trap and into many foolish and harmful desires that plunge people into ruin and destruction. For the love of money is a root of all kinds of evil. Some people, eager for money, have wandered from the faith and pierced themselves with many griefs. —1 Timothy 6:7–10*

I've never seen a hearse followed by a moving truck. We will not take anything from here to heaven. The only thing we can take to heaven is the reward, the result of our service in God's kingdom.

Everything Belongs to God

> *The earth is the Lord's, and everything in it, the world, and all who live in it.* —Psalm 24:1

God is the creator, sustainer, and controller of the entire universe. Everything belongs to Him.

We Must Properly Administer the Resources on Loan from God

> *The Lord God took the man and put him in the Garden of Eden to work it and take care of it.* —Genesis 2:15

God temporarily lends us goods so we can administer them. This administration includes the correct use of our material resources and the obedience to God's direction in relation to how we use them. We must learn and teach what biblical prosperity means—true prosperity is living in the center of God's will.

In the Hebrew language, the word for prosperity is *Shalom*, which has several meanings, including peace, welfare, health, and prosperity. In the Greek language, the word is *euodoo*, which gives the idea of being well guided, being on a good path, and being successful.

Prosperity may be linked to economic situations, but in the general context of the word of God, the term carries the idea of being in the center of the will of God.

The Challenge of Mind Renewal

The reality is that people not only in the Latin American continent but also in many parts of the world have a problem in the area of ownership and selfishness. One of the first words we learn as a child is "mine," and this possessive pronoun is used throughout our life, incorporating the idea that we really own things.

The systems of this world further imprint on people's minds the idea that ownership and happiness are synonymous. And so, the more we have, the more we want. The Bible, on the other hand says, "Whoever loves money never has enough; whoever loves wealth is never satisfied with their income. This too is meaningless" (Ecclesiastes 5:10). According to Solomon, the wisest man who ever lived, it is very difficult to find a rich person who is satisfied with what they have.

The norms and values of our society pressure us to believe that we need to have more: more financial assets, more powerful positions, and greater self-affirmation.

The biblical reality, as we have seen, is that God owns everything. It becomes clear that we do not have absolute ownership of anything. Again Solomon says, "Everyone comes naked from their mother's womb, and as everyone comes, so they depart. They take nothing from their toil that they can carry in their hands" (Ecclesiastes 5:15).

There is a vicious cycle that links the desire for wealth with the pursuit of power and position. Instead of producing happiness, this cycle is a downward spiral into a bondage of the spirit.

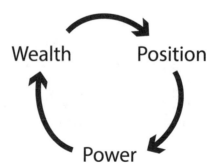

As we have seen in this book, when we understand and apply the principles of Christ-centered generosity, we will be set free from the bondage of ownership.

Beyond the bondage of thinking we own something, there is the equally misleading idea that happiness comes from material goods. The media, advertisements, and our world's values bring so many to press to possess things. We must beware of the inversion of values between this kind of thinking and the values of the kingdom of God. The apostle Paul, after his encounter with Christ, knew the sublimity of his Lord when he said, "What is more, I consider everything a loss because of the surpassing worth of knowing Christ Jesus my Lord, for whose sake I have lost all things. I consider them garbage, that I may gain Christ" (Philippians 3:8).

If we are to change this mentality in our people, we need to consider the following two things.

The Spiritual Is Worth More than the Material

The Christian who recognizes that the spiritual is more valuable than the material has a great deliverance from the bondage of ownership. Paul teaches the church, "So we fix our eyes not on what is seen, but on what is unseen, since what is seen is temporary, but what is unseen is eternal" (2 Corinthians 4:18). All that our eye can see one day will be destroyed, but the spiritual values are eternal.

Our Mind Needs to Be Renewed

The apostle Paul, recognizing the existence of reversed values, and also the pressure that the system of the world imposes on people, says:

> Therefore, I urge you, brothers and sisters, in view of God's mercy, to offer your bodies as a living sacrifice, holy and pleasing to God—this is your true and proper worship. Do not conform to the pattern of this world, but be transformed by the renewing of your mind. Then you will be able to test and approve what God's will is—his good, pleasing and perfect will. (Romans 12:1–2)

Note the exhortation is "Do not conform to the pattern of this world." The word "conform" has the idea of being shaped or framed. The system of this world tries to mold us into having this mindset, but the word of God urges us not to allow this. On the contrary, the text says, "but be transformed by the renewing of your mind."

It is the renewing of the mind that produces a change in behavior. To become free from the bondage of ownership, we need to have our mind renewed. This happens through the word of God and the presence of the Holy Spirit conforming us to the image of Christ.

I offer the following statement as a vision for the church in Latin America: *God owns everything and lends us the goods, the titles, and positions for a short time, and we must be responsible in properly administrating these benefits for His glory.*

A Call to Christian Leaders

Christian leaders in Latin America have a great challenge in helping their followers know and apply in their lives the concepts of Christ-centered generosity. As models for the people of God, we have first to live and teach this generosity ourselves. Then we must help our people to apply it in their own lives. Here are seven suggestions for a way forward.

Go Deeper in Study

Christian leaders should first know what the Bible teaches about Christ-centered generosity. This is a subject that has not received much emphasis in our churches. Therefore, leaders have a great opportunity to study and teach it boldly.

I did some research on the books being published by five leading Brazilian publishers, and only one had a book on stewardship. Much more needs to be written and preached on the subject from the perspective of eternity, the sovereignty of God, and the smallness and temporality of human existence. The Bible is full with teachings on God's ownership of everything and the call to every Christian to recognize the power, sovereignty, and ownership that are God's and God's alone.

Be Living Examples

In addition to studying, every leader must live the principles of the Word. Leaders are the model for their followers. The apostle Paul said, "Follow my example, as I follow the example of Christ" (I Corinthians 11:1). If leaders experience the freedom of the faithful steward, they will become living witnesses to the joy of life free from the pressures of ownership and can lead their people to have the same kind of life.

Build Accountability

One of the factors that keeps people from giving generously is a lack of accountability. Some Christians do not contribute because they do not know where the money is going. There are leaders who ask for offerings but are not clear on the application of those offerings. Others ask for the offering for one cause but apply it to another.

The offerings must be driven according to the word of God, and the leaders must make it clear where the funds will be applied. Clear accountability gives the church confidence in the leadership team, which produces a significant increase in generosity.

In my church I often give my people the opportunity to participate when important situations come up. On one such occasion, a couple from our church was serving in a Muslim country and needed a van for the ministry because they were depending on others for their transportation. I mobilized the church to give a special offering so we could purchase the vehicle. On that Sunday we raised all the money we needed. The people contributed with joy. Some months later, I showed the church on the projector a copy of the bank transfer receipt and the photo of the missionary couple in front of the van. The people clapped their hands, glorified God, and were pleased to have participated in the project. We were accountable every step of the way, and God blessed our people with the joy of generous giving.

Preach and Teach Christ-Centered Generosity

In addition to studying biblical stewardship and living generously, it is important to preach, teach, and admonish other people in this area.

Unfortunately, some leaders have taught the opposite. One leader in our nation, for example, is teaching that church members should honor their leaders by giving them expensive gifts, erroneously interpreting the verse "Give to everyone what you owe them: If you owe taxes, pay taxes; if revenue, then revenue; if respect, then respect; if honor, then honor" (Romans 13:7). Compounding the problem, these pastors are accepting their gifts without any accountability.

Some television programs sponsored by churches espousing prosperity theology show scenes of cars, boats, and luxurious mansions, saying that everything can be yours if you give generous offerings to the church. Attitudes like this fill people's hearts and minds with the concept that God blesses our thirst for ownership. The worst in this is that people are being exploited. The message of Christ-centered generosity has some enemies that must be fought and eliminated if we are to win back those hearts. They are greed, covetousness, and jealousy.

Greed

"Greed" is defined as a strong desire to continually get more of something and as the urge or ambition for honor or wealth. God put this in the Ten Commandments: "You shall not covet your neighbor's house. You shall not covet your neighbor's wife, or his male or female servant, his ox or donkey, or anything that belongs to your neighbor" (Exodus 20:17).

Human beings have a selfish tendency to own and control things and people. But God condemns such attitudes, because He knows about the negative results that those attitudes promote in life.

Covetousness

Covetousness is the sordid attachment to money and things, accompanied by the immoderate desire to acquire and accumulate wealth.

The Bible has a series of verses condemning this behavior, and Jesus's teaching about the danger of accumulating wealth and trust says, "Watch out! Be on your guard against all kinds of greed; life does not consist in an abundance of possessions" (Luke 12:15).

Jealousy

Envy, or jealousy, is characterized by the desire to have or enjoy what someone else possesses. The word of God classifies such an attitude and behavior as the lack of spiritual maturity.

As we see in 1 Corinthians 3:3, "You are still worldly. For since there is jealousy and quarreling among you, are you not worldly? Are you not acting like mere humans?"

Envy is one of the major contributors to the lack of generosity. Instead of sharing what have, we become enslaved by the desire to have what other people possess. The solution for eliminating these enemies is to have a mature and growing spiritual life, described as follows in the word of God: "I have been crucified with Christ and I no longer live, but Christ lives in me. The life I now live in the body, I live by faith in the Son of God, who loved me and gave himself for me" (Galatians 2:20).

If I am crucified, it means that my ego is dead, and now I have no more personal and selfish desires. But the text not only says that my ego is dead, but it also says that now Christ lives in me. This means a radical exchange: my wishes exchanged for the desires of Christ. Not my will, but his will; not my plans, but his. If this really happens in our spiritual life, we will live according to God's will and be free from the bondage of ownership.

Be Good Stewards

Now that we understand that everything comes from God and we have been delivered of the bondage of ownership, we need to have correct attitudes related to the goods that are lent us by God. The material goods that are under our care should be well managed. We cannot waste or use them wrongly. Some people take good care of the things they say they have, but when it comes to the belongings of others, they tend to neglect them. For example, people who rent cars usually use them with less care then they would with their own. It is a matter of character.

Provide Opportunities for People to Live Generously

We must always understand that everything that comes to our hands is a temporary loan from God. In the matter of money, knowing that God will supply all of our needs, we should pray and ask what He wants us to do with His money.

In our church, in addition to the tithe and mission offerings, we frequently raise offerings to help with social work. Every week we give food baskets, clothing, and outerwear for needy families. And when there is a disaster, the church is mobilized to participate not only by making financial contributions but also by personally bringing comfort and help directly to people in need.

A few years ago, there was a big rain in one region of the state of Rio de Janeiro. Some mountains were literally soaked with water. There was a large landslide, which formed an avalanche of mud that came down the mountainside and mixed with a river that overflowed and covered many homes. More than one thousand people died, many were injured, and thousands lost their houses. The government provided shelter for families, and the general public was mobilized to help and make donations. Our church had the honor of participating with donations of clothing, nonperishable food, etc.

But I want to highlight the participation of the young people of the church. One of the church leaders saw that there were many children in shelters because schools had been destroyed. These children had to stop studying and became very sad. This leader knew the Pack a Shoebox project from Samaritan's Purse and challenged the youth and adolescents of the church to organize shoeboxes with toys and toiletries for children. It was gratifying to see these young people and adolescents leaving in two buses, carrying these gifts, and spending a day in those shelters playing with the kids and taking the love of Christ to those families.

The point here is that the church approved the project and gave its members the privilege and opportunity to participate. I continue to hear testimonies of people who were and have been blessed by God because they are participating in His work.

The Bible is clear when it says that God blesses and supplies our needs, especially as we contribute to missionary work. But we must have the right motivation, not expecting to get something in return but believing in the work of advancing the kingdom of God.

Have a Great Missionary Vision

The church that God gave me the privilege of shepherding has a great missionary vision, and its members are challenged to give monthly for the support of missionaries beyond their regular tithes. Some receive high salaries and others live on tight wages, but all give their offerings with joy. I believe this is due in part to being deliberate in teaching about giving and challenging church members to give generously to the support of missionaries.

I learned from Dr. Oswald Smith, former pastor of the Peoples Church in Toronto, Canada, about the Faith Promise Offering. This is an offering method based on chapters 8 and 9 of 2 Corinthians, where the apostle Paul is teaching the church about generosity and giving to help the poor Christians in Judea.

In these two chapters, we find fourteen principles of generosity and stewardship:

- The contribution should be independent of the economic situation (8:2).
- It should be made, if necessary, with sacrifice (8:3).
- Insistently they asked for the privilege of giving (8:4).
- It should be a result of consecration to God (8:5).
- It is not an obligation (8:8).
- It should be planned (8:10–11).
- It should be in accordance with the ability of each (8:12).
- Equality produces equilibrium in the distribution (8:13–15).
- Leadership should be administered with transparency (8:20–21).
- It could be promised in advance (9:3–5).
- It involves the law of sowing (9:6).
- It should be done gladly (9:7).
- God will meet the needs of those who give generously (9:10–11).
- It produces glory to God (9:12–15).

Dr. Oswald Smith calls this Faith Promise Offering. During the church missionary conference, all participants receive a card that is divided in two parts with the following words: *In dependence upon God, I promise to contribute monthly to the missionary work of our church in the amount of…*

I contextualized this method for our church, and I was impressed by how members contributed with joy beyond their regular tithes. In 2013, our church gave more than $400,000 USD for missionary work. For a church with 1,300 members in a country with an emerging economy, this seems to reflect a heart for giving. We have used this model for over thirty-five years, and each year we have seen an increase in missionary contributions.

In summary, if we are to cultivate a culture of generosity in Latin America, our leaders will need to commit to the following work:

- Pastors and leaders must go deep in their biblical studies on Christ-centered generosity.
- Pastors and leaders must be the first to apply it in their own lives because they are the model for their followers.
- Pastors and leaders must preach, produce Bible studies, and pass on the biblical principles of stewardship.
- Pastors and leaders must provide opportunities for people to give generously, presenting them with effective projects and other needs.
- Pastors and leaders must have a great missionary vision to promote the support and advancement of the kingdom of God.

Conclusion

Finally, we know that God owns all of the gold and silver and we are just administrators of the good things of God. So we need to go deep in the concepts of Christ-centered generosity and understand how to live it. The pattern of Christian life is clear. Look at what the Bible says in Ephesians 4:22–24: "You were taught, with regard to your former way of life, to put off your old self, which is being corrupted by its deceitful desires; to be made new in the attitude of your minds; and to put on the new self, created to be like God in true righteousness and holiness."

The moment we put off the old self and put on the new self, we will be free of the sense of ownership, and our mind will be directed by the will of God. The text says that the new self is created to be like God in true righteousness and holiness.

Christ-centered generosity is a life lived in accordance with the direction of the Holy Spirit. God puts all the resources in our hands so that we might give generously to help others and expand the kingdom of God.

Questions for Individual Reflection and Discussion in Small Groups

- How has humanism shaped your culture's view of generosity?
- When we are commanded not to "conform to the pattern of this world," what are the implications for Christ-centered generosity?
- Read through the list of the fourteen principles of generosity and stewardship. Which ones are your strengths, and which are the ones where you struggle the most? What will you do in your areas of weakness to be a more faithful steward?

A South African Generosity
Childhood Memory

BY SAS CONRADIE (SOUTH AFRICA AND UNITED KINGDOM)

I spent five of my most formative years as a child on a mission station in the northern part of South Africa. My dad was a missionary of the Dutch Reformed Church working among the Shangaan people of South Africa. He had many preaching points—some Sundays he preached seven or eight times in different towns and villages. We often went with him, but being children, hearing that many sermons in one day was extremely boring. But there was one year when we wanted to go for a few Sundays to each of the services. The reason was not because we suddenly enjoyed or understood my dad's sermons but because Dutch Reformed congregations in the area bought cake and cold drinks for the Sunday school children where my dad preached. *Much* cake and *delicious* cake!

My dad asked us to help to give cake and cold drinks to the Sunday school children. Looking back now after many years, this was perhaps the first example of Christ-centered generosity that I can remember. And it influenced my own perspective on generosity as well. I will never forget the joy in the eyes of the children when they received the cake and cold drink. They were poor children who might not have eaten cake again for the rest of the year. They received cake given by Christians who experienced sharing with others as a pleasure. And that gave me joy as I gave the children the cake.

As Jesus says in Matthew 25:35, "I was hungry and you gave me something to eat." By being generous to others, we do not only express Christ's generosity, but we are actually generous to him as well! Perhaps that is where the seed had been planted for what I am doing now, where

129

the focus of my life, work, and ministry is to help others to live generously. Giving cake to poor children on a Sunday morning in a remote
part of South Africa might not mean much, but that was my first small
lesson in Christ-centered generosity! At least it was more exciting than
my dad's sermon…

Christian Generosity from
the Perspective of an African Pastor

BY REV. DR. PHILIPPE OUEDRAOGO (BURKINA FASO)

Africans are generally known to be generous. In many African cultures, members of families give hospitality and respect to visitors, the elderly, the handicapped, and the vulnerable people. It is known among them that often they give their daily food and beds to others in need and go without just to show their generosity to others. This is Christ-centered generosity in essence embedded in their culture. This generosity among Africans goes beyond the spontaneous to a longer term where the head of the family offers land to others in need so that they can settle in and grow food and have pasture for their livestock. He will send relief food to family members or needy people in the village or his area. The community members collectively offer their time and skills and resources to repair the houses of the elderly and the people with special needs.

I am sharing this reflection from a native community level. In Sub-Saharan Africa this spirit of generosity goes across cultures. At the local church level, it is common to see visiting preachers receive gifts in kind such as chicken, sheep, fruits, and vegetables as love offerings from the church community they visited or served. Money may be rare, especially during the raining period or what we call "hard to make the ends meet," which goes from sowing the seed that is more or less the only cereal people possess to the period of the first fruits (June to September, depending on the year). Yet Christians are still very happy to share whatever they have with the visitors, especially church leaders who cared enough to come and minister to them.

I have illustrated this generosity from African church leaders in my book[42] narrating how as a church family, pastors have opened their homes to receive girls and women running from forced marriages and family persecution (exclusion) because they chose to become Christian and thus rejected the pledged husbands they did not consent to live with. Such and similar situations are happening right now as I write. Globally, some will interpret what I am saying as the role of the government. But where such services were not reinforced at a community level, and where the resources were not available to tackle such a need at the national level, pastors did not wait. They initiated such generous acts in favor of the needy for thirty to forty years in place of government initiatives. Such good initiatives were followed up by the Christian churches and non-governmental organizations across Africa. African Christians are doing it out of love for the Lord Jesus Christ, not looking for any return from the beneficiaries, as "they gave themselves first of all to the Lord, and then by the will of God also to us" (2 Corinthians 8:5).

Another concrete example is my father.[43] He knew very little of the Western style of life because he lived and worked on his farm and was dedicated to the life of the local church of his village. In the last years of his life, he gave a large portion of his farming land: one hectare to build a local church and two hectares to build a Christian school for the children of the villages, who are largely from Muslim backgrounds. He lived a happy and fulfilled life and was pleased to give back to the community what God gave to him.

These examples testify that Christians in Africa have a Christ-centered generosity that is shared differently, reminding us that donating money is only one way of giving. The church in Africa is blessed with different types of wealth, and we need always to keep in mind what Jesus said: "It is more blessed to give than to receive" (Acts 20:35).

42. Philippe Ouedraogo, *Female Education and Mission: A Burkina Faso Experience* (Oxford: Regnum Books International, 2014), 180.

43. Philippe Ouedraogo, "Transforming Communities through Education" in *Good News from Africa: Community Transformation through the Church*, ed. Brian Woolnough (Oxford: Regnum Books International, 2013), 89.

Having Enough

By Dr. Wilf Gasser (Switzerland)

With six siblings and my father being a factory worker, I grew up thinking we were a poor family. My perception changed when, as a teenager, I was privileged to travel to Communist Romania. I got to know a gypsy family who shared two rooms with fifteen people. But they had found Jesus, were exuberant in joy and thankfulness, and they had no notion of poverty whatsoever.

Years later I learned that no matter whether you are rich or poor, you can live your life under the constant influence of a spirit of poverty that tells you the lie: "You don't have enough." I have met individual Christians, families, and even whole churches who live under this lie. Rich *and* poor have to hear and learn that our generous heavenly Father wants His children to live in freedom and in a spirit of generous living and generous giving.

That's why the generosity issue is so crucial for the church of today!

My Story: From a Mother and Ministry Leader

By Nydia R. García-Schmidt (Mexico and United States)

I began learning about generosity at a very young age from my mother. My mother came to know the Lord through an evangelical Gospel tract given to her when she visited her deceased relatives on *Día de los Muertos* (Day of the Dead), a very important day in Mexican culture. My mother experienced many traumatic events in her childhood, losing a brother because of tuberculosis and a sister in a home fire accident. It was in this Gospel tract that she understood the sacrifice of Jesus for her and how He provided answers to her pain and meaning in life.

Growing up, I heard many times how thankful she was for salvation and the gift of God, His word, the congregation, and loving people she met at church. One habit she had was to always set aside the tithe, and she neatly organized each bill all facing the same direction. As she organized her money, her intent was to set aside what she would give back to God in gratitude for all His blessings. She would start listing all the good things we had: health, a home, salvation, peace, etc. To this day, she can be seen counting her money and setting aside her tithe while narrating all the good things she has received by grace from God. She is thankful and is eager to give back to God what is His. She does not only give the tithe but is also eager to give more in offerings, knowing that she will never be able to out-give God. She counts her blessings in health, peace, and understanding of God. All this has produced in her an enormous state of contentment and gratitude toward God and His many mercies.

This example has allowed me to form my understanding about generosity that is based on gratitude toward God. Mom felt God had forgiven her many sins, and this produced great love for Him. All this understanding and childhood experience has allowed me to see the resources I have as ones that belong to God. Often when we as a family consider whom to help, I don't think twice about it—I love giving. As a family we are able to help several people during the year, and we have been supporting a pastor in India for many years through a nonprofit organization.

One of our biggest joys is receiving the generosity of others. We are being helped through our many years of living by faith in our full-time ministry roles, by relatives and close friends who also give with generosity and gratitude to God, blessing us to continue serving God. My biggest disappointment is when I see that people from church hold on to their God-given resources with a closed hand as if they own their resources and are not merely managers. I am therefore eager for Christians to understand the biblical foundations of Christian stewardship and how we are only stewards of His resources.

As a mother who has been involved in full-time ministry and having three teenagers/young adults, practicing Christ-centered generosity means that my lifestyle and giving habits are Kingdom centered. As our sons begin to learn how to earn and manage their own resources, we teach and encourage them to set aside their tithes and offerings. We also teach them the importance of being good stewards of the resources God has given them. Recently our oldest son, now in the military, was wondering where to give, and we were happy when he came to us for advice and council. Developing Christ-centered generosity means living our lives in obedience to His guidance and giving with a grateful heart.

PART VI

The Seven-Day Generosity Challenge

This is not a book about the theory of generosity. The intent of each contributor is to challenge and inspire you to engage in a life of joyful, Christ-centered generosity. Some may ask: Just what does this life look like? Practically speaking, how do we take these lessons, examples, and reflections and put them to work in our life? To answer those questions, we are concluding this book with a Seven-Day Generosity Challenge. We have asked seven leaders of ministries, Christian networks, and churches to provide readers with a practical set of actions that you can use to engender greater generosity in your life. For each of the seven days, there is a Scripture, a teaching, and a challenge. Many of the challenges include additional resources for your use if you want to read and study further in each of these areas.

As you will see, taking this Seven-Day Generosity Challenge will involve freedom, trust, courage, action, readiness, change, and risk. Commit today to take this challenge and set aside a full week to put these disciplines to work in your life. We know that the result will not only be greater generosity but will also include the unique joy that comes from obedience to the Most High Giver!

Biblical Stewardship: The Foundation of All Generosity

BY DR. ZENET MARAMARA (PHILIPPINES)

Scripture

The earth is the Lord's, and everything in it, the world, and all who live in it. —Psalm 24:1

Teaching

God, the maker of heaven and earth, owns all of creation and all it contains, as the Psalmist declares. In His benevolence He has given us all the resources of the earth to use and to enjoy. God, however, never transferred ownership to people. He continued to be the owner, and we are merely stewards. This truth has far-reaching implications for the way we live our life and use the resources entrusted to us, including money and possessions, our work, our business, and everything else we have.

If God is the owner and we are stewards, then we have to follow the will and desires of the owner. This involves knowing the heart of God, surrendering to His will, and living out our purpose. Stewarding God's creation and the resources entrusted to us means that we can generously share with others whatever blessings we receive. Generosity is an overflow of the steward's grateful response to God, who freely showers us with daily abundance.

God bestows us with material things for our personal needs, and we can help those who have less in life. Biblical stewardship liberates the stewards and frees them toward generous living and not just generous giving. John Wesley lived off of 10 percent of his income and gave away 90 percent. Most of us give 10 percent or even less and keep the rest for ourselves.

Does God need our money? He owns the cattle on a thousand hills, and every animal in the forest belongs to Him. God does not need our money, but He teaches us to give to help us gain the freedom from the love of money and to depend wholly on Him. Practicing biblical stewardship guards us from selfishness, greed, and hoarding.

Do you remember the story of Elijah, the prophet of God, and the widow at Zarephath in 1 Kings 17:7–16? There was famine in the land for three years, and the Lord directed Elijah to go to the widow at Zarephath who would feed him. The widow only had the last measure of flour and oil for her and her son's last meal, but she was able to give it up sacrificially to feed Elijah.

Why was she able to give up her family's last meal to the prophet? Because the Lord prepared her heart, and she trusted in Him to provide for her and her son. God was faithful, and the supply of flour from the jar and the oil in the jug never ran out.

The biggest hindrance to generosity is that we think we are owners. But if we understand that we are merely trustees and that God is the ultimate owner, this will lead us to follow the heart and the will of God. It can change the way we live in this world and treat material wealth. What a liberating thought, that we do not own any of our possessions!

That can save us from a lot of worries and stress! God is able to provide and take care of our needs. Imagine a world where people freely give and share. One Christian executive I know is a fine example of a steward. He gives support for Christian ministries and people who come to him for help. He says, "I am only a signatory of the Lord's check."

Challenge for Day One
Our response to God's generosity is to begin to surrender today our love for our earthly goods and to put our trust in God, who gives generously all that we ask and need. God as owner is also provider. Our responsibilities are faithful obedience to His will and to carry out God's wishes. That includes pursuing His kingdom and His righteousness, and all the other things will be added unto us.

It takes a journey of faith to fully rely on God to carry out His promises, and the time to begin is now. As we daily experience His grace and provision, our faith grows.

Remember the last time you were prompted by the Holy Spirit to make a sacrificial gift. How did you respond? Pray today for the Spirit to prompt you again, and be ready to sense that prompting. Pray that God will give you a sensitive heart and a willing spirit. When that happens, do not be afraid to respond obediently, trusting that God is able to restock His resources. Obey, and then write down how it felt to trust God through your generous giving.

Here is your challenge:

- Read 1 Timothy 6:6–10 and Matthew 6:24.
- Pray for God to rid your heart of the love of anything but Him.
- Respond by creating a list of things you want God to help you set aside, that you may love God more completely. Lay them before Him and feel the chains fall away as you surrender them back to Him.

The God of Elijah who kept refilling the widow's jar of flour and oil is the same God we serve today.

Day One: *Today I ask God to set me free from the love of earthly things.*

Abraham: An Example of the Generous Life

BY RICHARD SAMUEL (INDIA)

Scripture

The Lord had said to Abram, "Go from your country, your people and your father's household to the land I will show you.

"I will make you into a great nation, and I will bless you; I will make your name great, and you will be a blessing. I will bless those who bless you, and whoever curses you I will curse; and all peoples on earth will be blessed through you."

So Abram went, as the Lord had told him; and Lot went with him. Abram was seventy-five years old when he set out from Harran. He took his wife Sarai, his nephew Lot, all the possessions they had accumulated and the people they had acquired in Harran, and they set out for the land of Canaan, and they arrived there.

Abram traveled through the land as far as the site of the great tree of Moreh at Shechem. At that time the Canaanites were in the land. The Lord appeared to Abram and said, "To your offspring I will give this land." So he built an altar there to the Lord, who had appeared to him.

From there he went on toward the hills east of Bethel and pitched his tent, with Bethel on the west and Ai on the east. There he built an altar to the Lord and called on the name of the Lord. —Genesis 12:1–8

Teaching

When we are talking about generosity and about being generous, I would like for us to study a generous way of life, from the word of God. Abraham's journey is full of the open-handed lifestyle. One cannot live a generous life without God in it—it is not something that you *do*; it is something that you *are*. It is in the deeper journey with God that we begin to open our hands. We will examine three incidents in the life of Abraham that not only encourage us to embark on a deeper journey with God but also remind us that generosity is an outcome of a deep relationship with God.

First, God calls Abraham from his country to an alien land far away where he would bless him. And so, in obedience Abraham goes forth from Ur to Canaan, and there God appears to him again and says that He will give this land that he's on to Abraham. In chapter 13 we see that there is strife between the herdsmen of Abraham and Lot, so Abraham tells his nephew Lot to choose the land of his choice as his own and that thereafter Abraham would relocate to another place away from Lot. We have to step back to see the enormity of this posture. Here is the man of promise giving away the land of promise to Lot! Imagine the conversations at the tents that night, beginning with Sarah, all the way to the herdsman who would have been feeling a definite sense of loss and of having been shortchanged. Enter the tents of Lot and his herdsman—what would have been the general conversation that night? It would have been upbeat and may have even been one of having outsmarted Abraham. Enter Abraham's own mind that night—it would have been one of questions, perhaps even doubt. Lot chose the watered ground that is so needed for the flocks, leaving Abraham with hard, rocky places.

All of this weighs on Abraham, and soon his eyes are looking down, despair written over his face. In his strongest generous moment, he is also in his weakest place...with doubts and perhaps even fears—and God knows that. And knowingly enough, God shows up, as if to say, "You did well, Abraham!" In chapter 13:14–17:

> The Lord said to Abram after Lot had parted from him, "Look around from where you are, to the north and south, to the east and west. All the land that you see I will give to you and your offspring forever. I will make your offspring like the dust of the earth, so

that if anyone could count the dust, then your offspring could be counted. Go, walk through the length and breadth of the land, for I am giving it to you."

As soon as Lot leaves, God outdoes Abraham's generosity and says, "I am making you the center. All the four directions are yours from where you are! Everything that you see is yours." Then He says to Abraham, "Walk all over this place, claim this, mark all over it, it is yours." It is almost like Abraham and God are trying to out-give each other!

The second incident is found in Genesis 14 where four foreign kings defeat the king of Sodom, and Lot and his family and possessions are captured and taken away. On hearing this, Abraham immediately takes his men along with his allies and chases the four victorious kings and their troops and defeats them beyond Damascus. Abraham leaves his shepherding grounds and brings Lot and his family back with their possessions. And the king of Sodom offers him the entire possessions of his kingdom in return for the people. But Abraham says, "No, take it all!" He is not there for gain. He came for Lot and his welfare. If he is to prosper, it will be from the hand of his Lord God alone. All else, he gives away. What a high road. God alone will be his provider, not man.

And yet, imagine the inner condition on returning back home. He has defeated four kings and their armies and angered the king of Sodom. He has made at least five kings his enemies! Yet before Abraham can fear, God speaks to him in apt words never heard before: "Do not be afraid, Abram. I am your shield, your very great reward" (Genesis 15:1). God is again saying, "Do not regret doing this. Keep on obeying me and I will take care of the rest. Continue to take the higher ground—don't settle for less! You can do this, Abraham. You are secured." Then we see God give him even more territory than promised before, all the lands from Egypt's river all the way to the river Euphrates. First Canaan and now all the lands surrounding Canaan!

Finally, we see shortly after the birth of the promised child that God wants Abraham to sacrifice Isaac on Mount Moriah. Immediately we see

Abraham obey God in this also. According to Genesis 22:3, Abraham rose "early the next morning." No questions, no wrangling over His will or the fact Isaac is His promised child. *No!* None of these. With Abraham, when God speaks, he obeys. And just as Abraham is about to do the unthinkable, God intervenes by providing a ram for the sacrifice. Abraham gives it all away, even his own son, the most precious thing in his life. And God saves and rewards. Then God blesses Abraham's generations like He has never before or since blessed any man. God acknowledges Abraham's faithfulness: "You have not withheld your son, your only son." It is no coincidence that God's only son was also given on that same mount on Moriah.

Challenge for Day Two

From these three lessons, we learn that: (1) just as Abraham gave Lot the choice of land and trusted God to provide in whatever was left to him, so God today asks us to give up control of the things we think we possess and trust Him to provide; (2) God alone is our provider, and we should not look to anyone else to play that role; and (3) no matter the sacrifice God may require, generosity will always be rewarded with joy and God's rich provisions.

Name one place where you need to give up control and trust God to provide, even when others take advantage of your generosity. Now turn it over to God and be at peace in Him. Name one person you are relying on to be your provider instead of God. Repent today of that misplaced trust and, like Abraham, ask God to give you the strength and courage to trust in Him alone. Name one thing that God may be asking you to give away today in order to be obedient to His call to generosity. Make a decision today to be obedient, to give that thing away, and to watch God meet all of your needs.

Here is your challenge:

- Read 2 Corinthians 8:1–7.
- Pray for a heart that trusts God above everything else.

- Respond by recalling the times when God has met your needs in surprising and amazing ways. Write them down and share them with someone as a testimony to God's faithful provision.

Day Two: *Today I ask God to help me give up control and begin to trust Him to be my Provider.*

Financial Stewardship:
One-Kingdom Generosity

By Mike O'Neill (United Kingdom)

Scripture

As Jesus looked up, he saw the rich putting their gifts into the temple treasury. He also saw a poor widow put in two very small copper coins. "Truly I tell you," he said, "this poor widow has put in more than all the others. All these people gave their gifts out of their wealth; but she out of her poverty put in all she had to live on." —Luke 21:1–4

Teaching

What does your "all" look like?

In these four short verses, we have one of the foundational models for joyful management of our finances, and it comes from a widow. Widows (and widowers) live with loss all the time. Beyond the immediate sense of loss, pain, and heartache is the ongoing struggle to overcome the absence of their husband (or wife)—a source of physical, emotional, spiritual, and practical (including financial) support. For a widow in the first century in particular, life could be treacherous.

By Luke 20, Jesus is approaching the last days of his life and is spending his time teaching many groups of people at the temple in Jerusalem: Pharisees, Sadducees, teachers of the law, and his disciples. Teaching is his priority.

But as he looks up, something even more important captures his attention. He sees an unnamed widow, probably invisible to others, stepping forward and giving absolutely all she has in trust to God. She places two coins *into* the treasury.

Let's pause for a minute to consider the impact of that one single act and the implication that has for how we approach our financial stewardship.

The temple storehouse and treasury was designed for two groups of people: the Levite priests (who could own no property so depended on the temple for their financial needs) and the poor, the widows and orphans. It was a mechanism by which they could receive financial support, an early social welfare system. Each recipient from the temple store was dependent on the joyous generosity of God's people.

Those who had much, gave. Those who lacked, received.

And then suddenly this widow turns the system on its head. By rights, she could have taken from the treasury, according to her need. But instead she gives!

Nobody notices but Jesus. He stops in his tracks, moved by the way the poor widow gives: he tells us she gives all she has. He emphasizes this word "all" by repeating it three times in his two-sentence directive to the disciples. She gives everything. Nothing is held back.

He also names the widow's gift as "the truth." Remember, the widow in the temple is not a parable or a nice story about how even the poor can give. This is a real event. In this real moment in a real time and place, Jesus stops what he is doing because he sees truth.

By highlighting her gift, he foreshadows his own coming gift, as Hebrews 12:2 states, "For the joy set before him he endured the cross, scorning its shame, and sat down at the right hand of the throne of God." It is through giving that we can experience this joy for ourselves, not just in the instant of the gift but also for all eternity.

William Borden was as real as the poor widow in Luke. But he was fabulously wealthy. As the incredibly wealthy heir to a large family fortune at the start of the last century, the young man wanted for nothing and had the world at his fingertips. In 1904, after graduating from high school, William decided to travel around the world before attending university. Seeing hurting people on his travels altered his plans and moved him to become a missionary. He wrote two words in the back of his Bible: "No reserves."

After graduating from Yale University, Borden turned down all job offers before him. In his Bible, he wrote two additional words: "No retreats." He went on to seminary and, after finishing his studies, set sail for China. Hoping to work with Muslims, he stopped in Egypt to study Arabic. There, he contracted spinal meningitis and, within a month, the twenty-five-year-old died.

Before his death, William had written two more words in his Bible.

Underneath the words "No reserves" and "No retreats" was written: "No regrets."

With limited resources, the overpowering desire for a widow/widower is often to hold on to what you have and never let go. With great resources, the first reaction to a need could be to write a check, send another for a task, or to give "just enough." But both William Borden and the unnamed widow let go and gave all. And this is what they have in common with Jesus.

Our unnamed widow guides us to the way that we should live and give. William Borden shows us that material wealth, or poverty, doesn't matter.

Challenge for Day Three

So what, then, does this mean for our own financial giving? Whether you have a little or a lot, a foundation of joyful giving comes from understanding what your "all" looks like.

Here is your challenge:

- Read Luke 12:15–20 and Matthew 13:44.
- Pray that God will help you define your "all." Write it down and lay it before God. Share it with the person closest to you in your life. Do they agree?
- Respond by committing together to step out in courage and turn it "all" over to Him, whatever that may require, trusting that He will provide for all of your needs.

The widow and the heir both knew their all. They each held it lightly, ready and willing to give it all in pursuit of the eternal joy that supersedes all earthly joy. An eternal joy that may cost all we have: "no reserves" and "no regrets."

Day Three: *Today I ask God to give me the courage to name my "all" and hold nothing back from His control in my life.*

Generous Living: Taking Initiative

BY KEHINDE OJO (NIGERIA)

Scripture

One day Elisha went to Shunem. And a well-to-do woman was there, who urged him to stay for a meal. So whenever he came by, he stopped there to eat. She said to her husband, "I know that this man who often comes our way is a holy man of God. Let's make a small room on the roof and put in it a bed and a table, a chair and a lamp for him. Then he can stay there whenever he comes to us."

One day when Elisha came, he went up to his room and lay down there. He said to his servant Gehazi, "Call the Shunammite." So he called her, and she stood before him. Elisha said to him, "Tell her, 'You have gone to all this trouble for us. Now what can be done for you? Can we speak on your behalf to the king or the commander of the army?'"

She replied, "I have a home among my own people."

"What can be done for her?" Elisha asked.

Gehazi said, "She has no son, and her husband is old."

Then Elisha said, "Call her." So he called her, and she stood in the doorway. "About this time next year," Elisha said, "you will hold a son in your arms."

"No, my lord!" she objected. "Please, man of God, don't mislead your servant!"

But the woman became pregnant, and the next year about that same time she gave birth to a son, just as Elisha had told her. —2 Kings 4:8–17

Teaching

It is not unusual for a prophet of Elisha's status to have people who come to him primarily for what they can get, whether spiritual, material, or any kind of support. What he may not be familiar with are people who show acts of kindness and generosity without expecting anything in return. However, this is exactly what he gets and even more on a trip to Shunem. When the wealthy woman invites him in for a meal, he may think she or a member of her family has a problem that money cannot solve. It could be a need for deliverance, healing of a chronic disease that has defied medical care, or whatever. It is certainly a spiritual intervention of some sort.

Rather than asking for support of any kind from the man of God, this family takes the initiative to make their resources available to him by offering him a meal after a tiring journey. This invitation of guests—or, better put, strangers—to meals appears to be a norm for this family such that "no, thank you" was not an acceptable response. Therefore, she persuaded (*subtly forced*) Elisha to eat (2 Kings 4:8a)! Wow! She is giving away her meal, and she is not ready to take no for an answer. What a generous spirit! It appears that the meal must have been very rich and the atmosphere so cordial and hospitable that Elisha soon becomes a regular guest at meal tables in this home whenever his itinerary allows.

The woman, in consultation with her husband, then decides to take their generosity even further by building a guest chalet for Elisha. They are willing to release their resources freely to build and furnish a chalet for an itinerant minister. It is amazing how thorough they are in providing essential furnishings in order to guarantee a comfortable stay for their guest.

It is important to state that while people are still giving to causes in today's world, not all donations are made with pure and sincere motives. Elisha may have thought that sooner or later, this family would make their request, but to his amazement, they have no other motive than serving God's purpose and becoming a blessing to anyone who comes around their vicinity. When Elisha presses further to know why they have shown such generosity, the woman states categorically that she and her family dwell in a safe and secure environment. Their generosity is borne out of freewill and primarily to serve. What amazing freedom they enjoy in their giving.

They challenge us to remember that individuals, families, or institutions are to give in order to add value rather than focus on what they get back in return for their giving.

This particular story brings to light another key principle in generous living. This couple took the initiative to give, not because they were asked. It appears they were always looking for opportunity to make a difference. This virtue can be emulated by all, irrespective of cultures or circumstances.

Challenge for Day Four
Generosity involves both heart commitment and hand involvement. We are called to act on our convictions. In Elisha's story a family took the initiative, and they acted out their generosity in tangible ways. And we are called and privileged to do the same.

Prayerfully choose an individual, family, mission agency, or good cause that needs any kind of support or acts of kindness. It may involve the use of your talent, time, or treasure. You may want to make a visit, buy a gift, offer a service, provide counsel and/or encouragement, give a donation, pray, offer a meal, and so on. Reach out *today* to such persons, families, or organizations as guided by the Holy Spirit and act on the guidance that you have received.

Here is your challenge:

- Read 1 Timothy 6:17–19.
- Pray for God to give you joy in making a sacrificial gift.
- Respond by obeying what God puts in your heart. You may want to do any or all of the following in order to sustain this drive and be committed to generous living.
  - Create a fund for missions.
  - Decide who benefits from the fund.

- ○ Make a commitment to support your choice on a regular basis whether or not the needs are communicated to you.
- ○ Challenge friends, family, and your network to do the same.

Day Four: *Today I choose one person or ministry, and I will make a sacrificial gift of time, talents, or treasure as God leads.*

Strategic Generosity

BY GARY WILLIAMS (AUSTRALIA)

Scripture

Be very careful, then, how you live—not as unwise, but as wise, making the most of every opportunity, because the days are evil. —Ephesians 5:15–16

Teaching

A famous saying tells us, "Give a man a fish, feed him for a day. Teach a man to fish, feed him for a lifetime." Giving a fish and giving a fishing lesson are both small and simple acts of generosity but with vastly different outcomes. Development organizations have long recognized the strategic relevance of this concept. A spirit of generosity is wonderful, but it can become something truly transformational when we get strategic!

In Ephesians, Paul tells us to "be very careful" how we live. The phrase implies the ideas of observation, thoughtfulness, and focus beyond the normal. "Making the most of every opportunity" extends this concept further. Not just recognizing an opportunity, not just making something of it, but squeezing the absolute maximum out of it! And not just occasionally—every opportunity!

Early in my ministry, I applied for a grant from a foundation that I knew supported the concept of what we were doing. I was hopeful of receiving $10,000 or maybe even a bit more. Their considered response: "We'll give you $10,000 now, and if you can raise another $10,000 from other sources, we'll match that with another $10,000."

First, I was blessed by their generosity. We had a vision, and they were glad to respond. But I was doubly blessed (triply, in fact!) because of their strategic generosity. We were able to use their gesture to challenge other people to respond to our need, and we ended up with $30,000. But guess what? We weren't the only ones who were blessed. The other donors were excited that their gift had been strategically doubled, and the original donor was encouraged to see additional support emerge for us. And our mission was significantly advanced.

This is a simple and common example of strategic generosity. At the other end of the complexity scale, smart and generous people are doing amazing things by blending investment, generosity, and pseudobanking. Just pause and ponder, for a moment, the opportunities presented by things like low-interest housing loans, or leveraging the trillions of dollars that are sitting in the retirement funds of Christians around the world, or microenterprise support in the developing world. Strategic generosity is nothing new, but we still haven't begun to tap the potential that exists when we prayerfully seek to make the most of every opportunity.

Paul's instruction applies to all of us regardless of our wealth, our sophistication, or our circumstances. Maybe you are already living a careful life as a Christian, and that's great. But it may still be worth taking a moment to consider if we can be even more strategic.

Before we can make the most of an opportunity, we need to recognize it. It is not uncommon for us, busily engaged in all sorts of tasks and duties, to pass by an opportunity completely without even realizing it. Imagine, for a moment, that we were to have a debrief with God at the end of each day, when He could alert us to opportunities that we failed to recognize and thus failed to act on in the course of our day. If we had to give a daily account of missed opportunities, we might begin to be more alert to them when we encounter them.

Right now, stop for a couple of minutes and think back over the last week. Looking through the lens of "opportunities to be generous," can you recall anything that, in hindsight, may have presented an opportunity that you missed? (I just did this exercise myself, and yes, I missed a great opportunity six hours ago. By God's grace, I may be able to fix it before it's too late.)

If you, like me, discover that you have failed to even recognize opportunities, don't be discouraged. Act if you think you need to, but use this knowledge to inform your prayers in the days ahead. Developing a habit of recognizing opportunities to be generous is a necessary starting point. Of course, we don't need to wait for opportunities to drop out of the sky—we can also create opportunities whenever we like.

Identifying an opportunity, however, is just the first step. The exciting part comes next: What are we going to *do* about it? We have some options. We can deliberately ignore an opportunity. We can respond intuitively. Or we can respond strategically.

Challenge for Day Five

By way of challenge, I will suggest three simple disciplines that we can build into our daily life that can assist us to embody what Paul was talking about.

Here is your challenge:

- Read 2 Corinthians 9:6–12.
- Pray that God will reveal to you a new opportunity to give of your time, talents, and treasures to serve His kingdom. Pray daily that God will open your eyes to the opportunities He sends your way. When you recognize a specific opportunity, thank God for it, and then pause to ask for wisdom about how to respond. Sometimes a simple and spontaneous response is entirely sufficient, but sometimes, something more strategic may emerge upon consideration. Be sure to have periods during the year when you take extra time away to be with God, to seek His guidance, and to listen purposefully for His voice. During these times, think and pray specifically about how you can make the most of the opportunities that God gives you. This is where you get to be a proactive steward, not just a reactive one!
- Respond by immediately acting on the new opportunity, not delaying

it, practicing generosity as soon as the opportunity presents itself. Find a friend or a small group that you can talk with about these issues.

Next time you are presented with a clear opportunity for generosity, carefully assess whether this is a "fish" opportunity or a "fishing lesson" opportunity. Don't just make something of the opportunity—make the most of it! For the sake of the Kingdom.

Day Five: *Today I will look for one new opportunity to live generously, and I will act on it as God leads.*

Creation Care Is a Matter of Life

BY THE STAFF AND BOARD OF
THE EVANGELICAL ENVIRONMENTAL NETWORK (UNITED STATES)

Scripture

Jesus replied: "Love the Lord your God with all your heart and with all your soul and with all your mind." This is the first and greatest commandment. And the second is like it: "Love your neighbor as yourself." All the Law and the Prophets hang on these two commandments. —Matthew 22:37–40

Teaching

Creation care is a matter of life. The Evangelical Environmental Network (EEN) has been using that slogan for several years, and we have come to believe that it hits at the heart of the rationale for taking care of this earth and its inhabitants, including our neighbors. Here is what this phrase means to us.

First, it calls us to be champions and protectors of life. We do so in the name of the Lord and giver of life and for the sake of the author of life whom we love and serve. Being created in the image of God requires us to love life in every form as God created and sustains it. From conception through final breath, life must be seen as a precious gift from God that is to be stewarded and protected.

Second, it links our actions and attitudes toward creation with this mandate to be life protectors. Creation care means adopting a lifestyle that bears witness to our stewardship responsibility for this earth, a life modeled after the teachings of our Lord Jesus Christ. Such a life recognizes that all things were made by Him and for Him, and thus we need to consider how Jesus would have us steward what He made. This means cultivating attitudes that make us sensitive to the ways in which we contribute to the earth's degradation and pollution. Most importantly, it calls us to be proactive, intentional, and committed to speaking in our churches and communities as life protectors.

Third, it fills out Jesus's command to love our neighbor more holistically. It reminds us that we cannot love our neighbor and destroy the very environment that sustains our neighbor. This is especially true of our poor neighbor. The effects of a polluted planet hit the poor first and hardest. Rising sea levels, loss of arable land, drought, disease caused from pollution, and changing growing seasons are all devastating to our subsistence-level neighbors. Our decisions and actions every day with respect to creation care bear witness to the extent to which we truly love our neighbor as Jesus commanded.

Creation care *is* a matter of life. To be fully pro-life, we must understand the link between a degraded planet and the quality of life for so many of our neighbors.

As God's people, we must be careful to avoid two mistakes when it comes to understanding our role and responsibilities as image bearers of our creator God. The first is the error or shifting from creation care to earth worship. We worship the Father in the name of the Son by the power of the Spirit. Whenever divinity is bestowed on creation, it becomes an idol. While we must take seriously God's pronouncement that what He created is "very good," He never intended it to become the focus of our adoration. In the face of this error, we must repeat the words of Jesus to the enemy, "Worship the Lord your God, and serve him only" (Matthew 4:10).

The second error is to believe that creation is there for us to use as we wish without regard for our stewardship call. This error comes either from a mistaken definition of dominion or from an eschatological belief that it is all going to be burned up in the end anyway. Both views devalue creation and find no support in scripture. They stem instead from an erroneous, post-fall view of God's created intent for us. They demean creation and deny that the earth was created not for our domination but for us to nurture, steward, and use wisely.

Nowhere in scripture is our original mandate to tend the garden rescinded for a utilitarian, consumerist attitude toward creation. This is the error of owners who thirst for control and see all the earth's resources as consumable goods that they use even to their own detriment and that of their neighbor. Would God give us a mandate to use His good resources in a way that hurts our neighbor? Certainly not. Creation care requires humility and a servant's heart. It requires lives lived with the understanding that "the earth is the Lord's, and everything in it, the world, and all who live in it" (Psalm 24:1).

Once we avoid these two errors and we see the link between creation care and loving our neighbor, we can assume the mantel of the generous, faithful steward with regard to our relationship to God's good earth. We can protect life, love our neighbor, and care for creation as a central part of our life as a disciple of Jesus Christ.

Challenge for Day Six

So what are God's people to do if we are to live out Jesus's command holistically? We offer a three-fold challenge to get us started—or to take us further.

Here is your challenge:

- Read Psalm 24:1–5.
- Pray for wisdom to see where your lifestyle is damaging God's creation and for courage to change.
- Respond by:
    o Declaring God's ownership: Please take this seriously, as it will be an attitude-shifting event. Collect everything in your life that represents ownership and relationship. Things like your house deed, car title, stock and retirement documentation, kids' birth certificates (yes, that's right), marriage license, will, bank account balances…you get the idea. Now, with everything stacked up, lift

it up in prayer and surrender it all back to God. He owns it anyway. So use this as a reminder that it's all His—all of it, including your relationships. As you surrender it back to Him, see if you don't feel a sense of freedom as if chains fall. That is the freedom of the faithful steward.

o Starting a discussion: Gather a group of people from your church or work and commit to going through Scripture and asking God to guide you in understanding your role as stewards of creation. There are a number of great resources to help guide you, and we have listed several in the resources section. As you study the word of God, be ready to be surprised, challenged, and inspired to engage in creation care at a whole new level.

o Changing one habit: As a result of number one, surrendering everything to God, and number two, discovering what God's word says about caring for creation, make a commitment to identify one habit in your life that needs to be changed or eliminated. It may be a consumer habit, a polluting habit, or an apathy habit. Whatever the Spirit brings to your awareness, commit today to change or eliminate it, and replace it with a positive action that bears witness to your new passion for creation care. If you change one habit, you will open the pathway for deeper reflection and the continuing work of the Holy Spirit in you as you seek to be a more faithful steward of creation and all of life. To God be the glory!

Day Six: *Today I will change one habit so that my life will better reflect my love for my neighbor through my care for God's creation.*

The Generosity Roller Coaster: Forty Days of Generosity

By Pastor Rony Madrid (Guatemala)

Scripture

This is the kind of fasting I want: Free those who are wrongly imprisoned; lighten the burden of those who work for you. Let the oppressed go free, and remove the chains that bind people. Share your food with the hungry, and give shelter to the homeless. Give clothes to those who need them, and do not hide from relatives who need your help. —Isaiah 58:6–7

Teaching

If you want to have real fun, you must ride the generosity roller coaster. I live in Guatemala, a country with many challenges. But maybe the biggest challenge is to be able to see what the Lord sees and do what the Lord wants. There is so much poverty here that those who were born here have learned to accept it as part of the landscape. I am pastor of a church called Real Life, and through verses in Isaiah 58, the Lord began to awaken my heart to help the needy. In this passage, God says to His people, "I'm not impressed with your religion if you do not dedicate yourself to help the poor."

As a result of understanding the will of God, we decided to start a movement called Iniciativa58 and also to do a nationwide campaign called 40 Days of Generosity. We wanted to teach churches and Christians across Guatemala the blessing of giving and to show God's love for needy people in our country. Brian Kluth, founder of Loving Our Community, gave us permission to use his *40 Day Generous Life* devotional across Guatemala. We had a vision event and challenged pastors to give out the devotional, to preach on generosity, and to invite families to read the devotional together every day. At the end of the forty days, we asked each church to raise the greatest offering that they had ever collected. But to do this with pure motives, the offerings that churches received were to go to help the needy. Over one hundred churches, denominations, ministries, businesses, and groups decided to join the 40 Days of Generosity for our country.

Also my friend Jaime Farrach, a well-known businessman in my city, was able to arrange for free advertising space on TV, radio, and newspapers. These 40 Day ads were to challenge all Guatemalans to be more generous. What a joy to see how the Lord opened this media door for us, as $4,000 USD in advertising was donated for this project!

The Lord was also working behind the scenes. One month before the campaign started, my friend Dave Polstra from Perimeter Church in Atlanta came to Guatemala. He told me that his church had a matching fund of $20,000 USD to help build houses for people in need. This proposal came precisely at the time when we were deciding how my church's 40 Day offering could be used to help the needy. We felt that God was calling us to allocate our offering to build houses.

In Guatemala there is an organization called Un Techo para Mi País ("A Roof for My Country") that uses volunteers to build small houses for $1,500 USD each. We decided to challenge our church families to give their offerings to help build houses for needy families.

At the beginning I thought we could raise the $20,000 USD, meet the matching fund, and build twenty-five or more houses. During the campaign my faith grew, and I thought we could raise enough money to build forty to sixty houses. On the day of the offering, we were surprised by the Lord. We saw many families make enormous efforts to generously support this project.

Here are just a few examples of the outpouring of generosity we experienced:

- A young girl asked her dad to donate all of her quinceañera celebration monies (a long-awaited and costly family event for teenage girls in Latin America when they turn fifteen) to build houses for the needy.
- A grandparent couple had been saving up money to take all of their grandchildren to Disney World. When the 40 Day campaign happened, the grandchildren came to the grandparents and asked them to donate all the Disney World vacation monies to help build houses for the needy. One of the eight-year-old grandsons said, "Grandpa, if God wants us to go to Disney World someday, He will provide another way. But these families need our help now."
- A Christian businessman challenged all his employees to donate and help build houses for the needy. He told them he would double whatever funds they gave. The employees pooled their resources and raised $15,000 USD, and he matched it with another $15,000—and together their company helped build twenty houses.

When the forty days were over, we didn't receive a $20,000 offering or a $40,000 or $60,000 offering. When all the offering monies were counted at our church, we received $469,000 USD—enough to build 312 houses! This was the greatest offering our church had ever received in one event. We praise the Lord for what He did in us and through us during these forty days.

The next year, the Lord again put in my heart the idea that we should do another campaign to help the needy. At first I had my doubts if this was a good idea. I was afraid that maybe people were getting tired of giving. But one morning, I received an e-mail from a lady in the congregation. She knew nothing about the idea that God had put into my heart. She wrote me, "Good morning, Pastor Rony. God bless you and your ministry. I want to give you a message from the Lord: He told me about a health campaign that is in your heart. He says, is not from you, He has placed in your heart. Don't worry, because He has it all planned."

This was remarkable because at that time, this was not something that many people knew about. God used this woman's e-mail to confirm for me that this was all God's idea. As we moved forward, we decided we wanted to bless people living in extreme poverty with four basic items they needed for their health and well-being:

- Water filter: Contaminated water is the major cause of chronic malnutrition in Guatemala. Fifty-two percent of the population suffers from this condition.
- Ecological stove: Many mothers get sick and even die from lung diseases because they cook using open fires.
- Solar panel with four lights: In Guatemala, many houses do not have electricity.
- Ecological latrine: These help avoid contamination that they might be at risk for with less sanitary facilities.

This time we did the campaign only at my local church. But again we had so much fun doing this together. As a result the Lord allowed us to help one thousand families with a kit called Home Health. At this time we are sending teams of volunteers to bless many families with these Home Health kits.

Challenge for Day Seven
It's fun to be generous. In this short article, I cannot tell about all the miracles we saw in the process. What I can do is invite you to have fun on the generosity roller coaster, in which we obey God and see Him supernaturally provide.

Here is your challenge:

- Read Isaiah 58:5–7.
- Pray for a new vision for your generosity. Hear from God. Pray with an open heart that God will lead you in one specific area of generosity. Perhaps He has had it in your heart for a while and now is the time to step out in faith. Don't stop praying until you know with certainty what God wants you to do.
- Respond to what God puts in your heart, and be prepared to be challenged and blessed. Take a risk in being generous. This is your part of

the roller-coaster ride. Step out in faith and be obedient to what God has put in your heart. If it is from Him, it will likely require trust, faith, and courage. Don't hold back—step out and do what He has put in your heart to do. See how He guides and provides. Expect God to meet your needs, but also expect to be surprised. Watch how He will multiply your generosity and perhaps call you into an even deeper level of generosity as a result. Remember, it is a roller coaster. Enjoy the ride!

Day Seven: *Today I will take a risk and act generously in a new way as God leads.*

Challenge for Day One: Freedom

Today I ask God to set me free from the love of earthly things.

- Read 1 Timothy 6:6–10 and Matthew 6:24.
- Pray for God to rid your heart of the love of anything but Him.
- Respond by creating a list of things you want God to help you set aside, that you may love God more completely. Lay them before Him and feel the chains fall away as you surrender them back to Him.

Challenge for Day Two: Trust

Today I ask God to help me give up control and begin to trust Him to be my Provider.

- Read 2 Corinthians 8:1–7.
- Pray for a heart that trusts God above everything else.
- Respond by recalling the times when God has met your needs in surprising and amazing ways. Write them down and share them with someone as a testimony to God's faithful provision.

Challenge for Day Three: Courage

Today I ask God to give me the courage to name my "all" and hold nothing back from His control in my life.

- Read Luke 12:15–20 and Matthew 13:44.
- Pray that God will help you define your "all." Write it down and lay it before God. Share it with the person closest to you in your life. Do they agree?
- Respond by committing together to step out in courage and turn it "all" over to Him, whatever that may require, trusting that He will provide for all of your needs.

Challenge for Day Four: Action

Today I choose one person or ministry, and I will make a sacrificial gift of time, talents, or treasure as God leads.

- Read 1 Timothy 6:17–19.
- Pray for God to give you joy in making a sacrificial gift.
- Respond by obeying what God puts in your heart. You may want to do any or all of the following in order to sustain this drive and be committed to generous living.
    - Create a fund for missions.
    - Decide who benefits from the fund.
    - Make a commitment to support your choice on a regular basis whether or not the needs are communicated to you.
    - Challenge friends, family, and your network to do the same.

Challenge for Day Five: Readiness

Today I will look for one new opportunity to live generously, and I will act on it as God leads.

- Read 2 Corinthians 9:6–12.
- Pray that God will reveal to you a new opportunity to give of your time, talents, and treasures to serve His kingdom. Pray daily that God will open your eyes to the opportunities He sends your way. Be sure to have periods during the year when you take extra time away to be with God, to seek His guidance, and to listen purposefully for His voice.
- Respond by immediately acting on the new opportunity, not delaying it, practicing generosity as soon as the opportunity presents itself. Find a friend or a small group that you can talk with about these issues.

Challenge for Day Six: Change

Today I will change one habit so that my life will better reflect my love for my neighbor through my care for God's creation.

- Read Psalm 24:1–5.
- Pray for wisdom to see where your lifestyle is damaging God's creation and for courage to change.
- Respond by:
    - Declaring God's ownership by putting all of the documents that symbolize your ownership of things (deeds, titles, financial reports, etc.) on a table and then praying over them, surrendering everything back to God.
    - Starting a discussion. As you study the word of God, be ready to be surprised, challenged, and inspired to engage in creation care at a whole new level.
    - Changing one habit. If you change one habit, you will open the pathway for deeper reflection and the continuing work of the Holy Spirit in you as you seek to be a more faithful steward of creation and all of life. To God be the glory!

Challenge for Day Seven: Risk
Today I will take a risk and act generously in a new way as God leads.

- Read Isaiah 58:5–7.
- Pray for a new vision for your generosity. Hear from God. Pray with an open heart that God will lead you in one specific area of generosity.
- Respond to what God puts in your heart, and be prepared to be challenged and blessed. Take a risk in being generous. This is your part of the roller-coaster ride. Step out in faith and be obedient to what God has put in your heart. Remember, it is a roller coaster. Enjoy the ride!

My Favorite Biblical Generosity Story

By R. Scott Rodin (United States)

It has been my joy and privilege to serve as an author and general editor of this book. I pray you have been blessed by what you have read. In concluding *Christ-Centered Generosity*, I want to share with you my favorite story of generosity from Scripture. I don't think it is often viewed as a story about faithful asking and generous giving, but the truth of both is clear. The story comes from Luke, chapter 19, beginning at verse 28:

> And after Jesus had said this, he went on ahead going up to Jerusalem. As he approached Bethphage and Bethany at the hill called the Mount of Olives, he sent two disciples, saying to them, "Go to the village ahead of you, and as you enter it, you will find a colt tied there, which no one has ever ridden. Untie it and bring it here. If anyone asks you, 'Why are you untying it?' say, 'The Lord needs it.'"
>
> Those who were sent ahead went and found it just as he had told them. As they were untying the colt, its owners asked them, "Why are you untying the colt?"
>
> They replied, "The Lord needs it."

Jesus sends his disciples ahead of him, telling them they are going to find a colt tied up in front of a certain person's house. They are to go up, untie the colt, and bring it to Jesus. He also tells them that if anybody comes out and asks them what they are doing, they are to say, "The Lord needs it." Armed with this directive, they go into Jerusalem.

We know from the history of that time that a colt was a very prized possession, one of the most valued possessions a household could own. It would one day serve as transportation and as a tool to pull a plow and carry items to market. In short, this young colt was going to play a major role in the health and prosperity of this family.

So these disciples come along and find the colt as Jesus said, and, as they were instructed, they start untying it and leading it away in broad daylight. The scripture says that the owners see all of this happening and respond with a simple question, "Why are you untying that colt?" That may be what they said, but I don't think that is *how* they said it. I think they likely picked up sticks and came running out at them, yelling in anger at the top of their lungs, "Why are you untying that colt?"

All the disciples say in response to the owners' protest is what Jesus instructed them to say: "The Lord needs it." The Lord needs it. We assume that the owners of the colt know who "the Lord" is and that the Lord is their Lord, too. And that is all that the owners need to hear. What a response of faith!

The owners of that precious colt do not need a direct mail fundraising letter. The disciples do not take out a brochure and say, "Well, this colt is part of the Triumphal Entry Campaign. As you'll see here by our table of gifts, we need five contributions at the colt level, and we are hoping you would consider giving one of those today." They offer no plaque on the walls of Jerusalem. No seat next to Jesus at the major donor banquet.

"The Lord needs it." That is all the disciples say to these angry owners brandishing sticks. And upon hearing those words, the owners just let it go. No promise is given of its return. They just let it go, all because the Lord needs it. What a marvelous picture of a heart tuned to God. Imagine what it must have been like for those owners in a few short hours to see the King of Kings and the Lord of Lords riding triumphantly into Jerusalem *on their own colt.*

I love this simple example of giving sacrificially for the right reason and then seeing what amazing things God does with that gift.

On behalf of all the authors of *Christ-Centered Generosity*, our prayer is that through the words and the challenges in this book, you have been led by the Holy Spirit to cultivate a more generous and obedient heart. As you do, expect God to bring before you great opportunities to invest in the work of the Kingdom. He will give you abundant opportunities to search your heart and ask yourself if God is saying to you, "I need you to share what I have given you, that this work may be completed." And we pray that you will respond obediently, which, in Kingdom terms, always means abundantly and joyfully. Just because the Lord needs it.

As a witness to the work that God will do in you and through you, we encourage you to read and sign the Generosity Declaration on the next page. It is time for God's people across the globe to step out in faith and live lives of extravagant generosity, bearing witness to our extravagantly abundant God.

To God be the glory!

My Commitment to Biblical Generosity

I affirm that:

- God is indescribably generous. We see this in His creation and experience it in His redemption plan through the life, death, resurrection, and ascension of Jesus Christ (John 3:16).
- God is creator, sustainer, and owner of all things (Psalm 24:1). He has supplied His infinite resources to us to steward for His kingdom purposes, including to reach the ends of the earth for the glory of His name (Luke 12:42–48; Revelation 7:9–12).
- Just as Jesus lived a truly and perfectly generous life to serve and save people (Mark 10:45, 2 Corinthians 9:8–9), it remains fundamental, therefore, that Christians model biblical service, generosity, and stewardship (Mark 10:45, 1 Corinthians 4:1, 2 Corinthians 9:8–9).

I therefore commit myself to foster a culture of biblical generosity and stewardship that will transform individuals and communities as I:

- Recognize that generosity is manifested in giving funds, resources, time, talents, gifts, prayer, and my very presence.
- Practice holistic stewardship, generous living, and gracious financial giving while encouraging these virtues within my sphere of influence through modeling, teaching, and equipping.
- Engage openly with other Christians and their networks in a global movement in which the whole church lives out and takes the whole gospel to the whole world as effective and generous stewards.

Name: _____

Signature: _____

Date: _____

Resources for Further Study

Books

Alcorn, Randy. *The Treasure Principle*. Colorado Springs: Multnomah Books, 2001.

———. *Money, Possessions, and Eternity*. Wheaton, IL: Tyndale House Publishers, 1989.

Blomberg, Craig L. *Heart, Soul, and Money: A Christian View of Possessions*. Joplin, MO: College Press, 2000.

———. *Neither Poverty nor Riches: A Biblical Theology of Material Possessions*. Grand Rapids, MI: William B. Eerdmans, 1999.

———. *Christians in an Age of Wealth: A Biblical Theology of Stewardship*. Grand Rapids, Michigan: Zondervan, 2013.

De Neui, Paul H., ed. *Complexities of Money and Missions in Asia*. Pasadena, CA: William Carey Library, 2012.

Elder, Brett and Stephen Grabill, eds. *NIV Stewardship Study Bible: Discover God's Design for Life, the Environment, Finances, Generosity, and Eternity*. Grand Rapids, MI: Zondervan, 2009.

Getz, Gene A. *A Biblical Theology of Material Possessions*. Chicago: Moody, 1990.

———. *Real Prosperity: Biblical Principles of Material Possessions*. Chicago: Moody, 1990.

Hall, Douglas John. *The Steward: A Biblical Symbol Come of Age*. Grand Rapids, MI: William B. Eerdmans, 1990.

Hoag, Gary G., and R. Scott Rodin. *The Sower: Redefining the Ministry of Raising Kingdom Resources*. Winchester, VA: ECFA Press, 2010.

Hoag, Gary G., R. Scott Rodin, and Wesley K. Willmer. *The Choice: The Christ-Centered Pursuit of Kingdom Outcomes*. Winchester, VA: ECFA Press, 2014.

Jabini, Frank S. *How to Give Joyfully*. Bryanston, South Africa: South African Theological Seminary Press, 2009.

Jeavons, Thomas H., and Rebekah Burch Basinger. *Growing Givers' Hearts: Treating Fundraising as Ministry*. San Francisco: Jossey-Bass, 2000.

Longenecker, Bruce W. *Remember the Poor: Paul, Poverty, and the Greco-Roman World*. Grand Rapids, MI: William B. Eerdmans, 2010.

MacDonald, Gordon. *Generosity: Moving Toward Life that is Truly Life*. N.p.: GenerousChurch, 2008.

Ramsay, Dave. *The Total Money Makeover*, Nashville, TN: Thomas Nelson, 2013.

Rodin, R. Scott. *The Million-Dollar Dime*. Spokane, WA: Kingdom Life Publishing, 2012.

———. *The Steward Leader: Transforming People, Organizations and Communities*. Downers Grove, IL: InterVarsity Press, 2010.

———. *Stewards in the Kingdom: A Theology of Life in All Its Fullness*. Downers Grove, IL: InterVarsity Press, 2000.

Smith, Gordon T. *Beginning Well, Christian Conversion and Authentic Transformation*. Downers Grove, IL: InterVarsity Press, 2001.

Tongoi, Dennis O. *Mixing God with Money: Strategies for living in an uncertain economy*. Nairobi, Kenya: Bezalel Investments Ltd., 2001.

Willard, Chris, and Sheppard, Jim. *Contagious Generosity: Creating a Culture of Giving in Your Church*. Grand Rapids, MI: Zondervan, 2012.

Websites and Online Resources

#1 Generosity Devotionals to Grow Givers and Giving, www.generosity devotional.com

40acts, "Do Lent Generously," www.40acts.org.uk

Dave Ramsay, Financial Peace Univeristy, http://www.daveramsey.com/fpu

Center for Congregations, "Stewardship and Generosity," www.center forcongregations.org/system/files/StewardshipGenerosity.pdf

Charities Aid Foundation, "Future World Giving: Unlocking the Potential of Global Philanthropy," www.cafonline.org/pdf/Future_World _Giving_Report_250212.pdf

GenerousChurch, www.generouschurch.com

Generous Giving, "Research Library," http://library.generousgiving.org/page.asp?sec=28&page=

Generosity Gameplan, http://generositygameplan.com/

Giving in Grace, www.givingingrace.org

Global Generosity Network, "Resources," http://community.generositymovement.org/en/resources

"Go" by Hillsong United, www.youtube.com/watch?v=9eHg8s8M4no

I Like Giving, www.ilikegiving.com

Issachar Initiative, Count for Zero Curriculum, www.issacharinitiative.org/count-for-zero

The Lausanne Movement (http://conversation.lausanne.org), particularly:

"Community Resources: Stewardship," http://conversation.lausanne.org/en/resources/browse/keyword/stewardship

"Community Resources: Generosity," http://conversation.lausanne.org/en/resources/browse/keyword/generosity, of note:

- Charities Aid Foundation, World Giving Index 2014
- Generosity Exercises, Gary Hoag
- Generosity Resources List
- The Generous Business: A Guide for Incorporating Giving at Work
- The Giving Journey: A Guide to the Joy of Generosity
- Kingdom Stewardship: Occasional Papers Presented for Cape Town 2010
- Missions Africa Trust Fund Ghana Consultation Press Release and Presentation
- The Money Revolution: Applying Christian Principles to Handling Your Money, John Preston
- Live Just.ly, www.livejust.ly/ (also a book: www.livejust.ly/product/live-justly-book)

Maximum Generosity (www.kluth.org), particularly:

"Wise Giving Q&A Series," www.kluth.org/Questions-on-charitable-giving-tithing-donations.htm

"Brian's Most Popular Devotionals, Books, and Manuals," www.brian
kluth.org/3-Brian-Kluth-Books-and-Products.htm
The Money Revolution, www.themoneyrevolution.net
Parish Resources, www.parishresources.org.uk
SEL France (www.selfrance.org), particularly:
"Découvrez le Parcours du Partage!" www.selfrance.org/index
.php?id=917
"Des Resources Pour Sensibliser," wwwselfrance.org/index.php?id=897
Southern Nazarene University, "No Reserves. No Retreats. No Regrets:
William Borden's Life,", http://home.snu.edu/~hculbert/regret.htm
Stewardship (www.stewardship.or.uk), particularly:
"BudgetBuilder," www.stewardship.org.uk/resources/budgetbuilder
"David Flowers: Setting a Budget," www.stewardship.org.uk/blog
/blog/post/293-david-flowers-setting-a-budget
"Resources," www.stewardship.org.uk/resources
"Seasons of Giving" Course, www.stewardship.org.uk/money/spotlight
/seasons-of-giving
"Stewards: Ten Lepers—Good or Bad Stewards?", www.stewardship.org
.uk/blog/blog/post/169-stewards-ten-lepers-good-or-bad-stewards/
Stewardship Summit, "Previous Summit Papers," www.stewardshipsum
mit.org/sessions/downloads.asp
The Steward's Journey, www.thestewardsjourney.com
Stewardship, *The Art of Giving* blog, "The T-Word," www.stewardship
.org.uk/blog/blog/post/160-the-t-word
Stewardship Ministries, "Useful Books," www.stewardshipministries
.org/resources/books
Web of Creation, www.webofcreation.org
YouTube, "Stewardship" Channel, www.youtube.com/stewardshipuk

Organizations, Academic Institutions, and Networks
Asian Theological Seminary, www.ats.ph/ws/academics/special-programs
/ats-center-for-biblical-stewardship
Canadian National Christian Foundation, www.cncf.ca

CBMC, http://www.cbmc.com/

CBMC International, http://cbmcint.com/

Center for Faith and Giving, www.centerforfaithandgiving.org

Christian Institute of Management, www.cimindia.in

Christian Leadership Alliance, www.christianleadershipalliance.org

Christian Management Australia (CMA), www.cma.net.au

Christian Stewardship Association Philippines, www.csaphils.com

Christian Stewardship Network, www.christianstewardshipnetwork.com

Compass, www.compass1.org

Crown Financial Ministries, www.crown.org

Cultura Financiera, www.culturafinanciera.org

Dave Ramsay, http://www.daveramsey.com/home/

Ecumenical Stewardship Center, www.stewardshipresources.org

Evangelical Council for Financial Accountability (ECFA), www.ecfa.org

The Gathering, www.thegathering.com

Generosity Monk, www.generositymonk.com

The Generosity Trust, www.thegenerositytrust.org

GenerousChurch, www.generouschurch.com

Generous Giving, www.generousgiving.org

Generous Journey, www.generousjourney.org.uk

Global Generosity Network, www.generositymovement.org

Good Sense, www.goodsensemovement.org

Gospel Bankers Inc., www.gospelbankers.com

Halftime Institute, www.halftimeinstitute.org

Helplift Network, www.helplift.co.za

International Steward, www.intsteward.org

Issachar Initiative, www.issacharinitiative.org

Kingdom Advisors, https://kingdomadvisors.org/Default.asp

Leadership Network, www.leadnet.org

Marketplace Ambassadors, http://www.marketplaceambassador.com

Maximum Generosity, www.kluth.org

Mission Supporters League, www.mslonline.org

National Christian Foundation, www.nationalchristian.com

National Generosity Network, www.generositynetwork.in
Royal Treasure, www.royaltreasure.org
SEL France, www.selfrance.org
Southwestern Baptist Theological Seminary Center for Biblical Stewardship,
    www.swbts.edu/academics/centers/center-for-biblical-stewardship
Stewardship, www.stewardship.org.uk
The Stewardship Alliance, www.stewardshipalliance.com
Stewardship Ministries, www.stewardshipministries.org
Stewardship of Life Institute, www.stewardshipoflife.org
Stewardship Summit, www.stewardshipsummit.org
Women Doing Well, www.womendoingwell.org

Contributor Biographies

Adijanto, Suparno
Suparno Adijanto, PhD, is CEO of Multimatics Group and Global Palm Resources Ltd. He lives in Jakarta, Indonesia, and serves on the boards of Crown Financial Ministry and Ichthus International School. He is also an elder of Jakarta International Christian Fellowship.

Adleta, Liz
R. Elizabeth Adleta is the executive director of Global Christian Network, Inc. and the Prayer Workgroup Co-Facilitator of the Ethnê Movement. She lives in Tulsa, Oklahoma, USA, and serves globally with the Global Ephesus Support Team. Also, Elizabeth is a field associate with Modern Day and International Partnering Associates.

Chavez, Luis
Luis Chavez was born in the state of Oaxaca and had been the Executive Chairman of Unión Nacional de Traductores Indígenas (UNTI) Mexico since 2009. UNTI is a union of indigenous Bible translators in Mexico. He belongs to a Zapotec family and is married to Bibiana Mendoza.

Chiang, Samuel
Rev. Samuel Chiang is executive director of International Orality Network. He was born in Taiwan and grew up in Canada. He currently lives in Hong Kong with his wife, Robbi. He serves on the board of the Seed Company.

Chung, Sung Wook
Sung Wook Chung, DPhil, is professor of Christian theology at the Denver Seminary and president of Kurios International, a global missional

organization. He lives in Highlands Ranch, Colorado, USA, and serves
on the boards of ZeroTB America and Servant of Harvest Ministry.

Conradie, Sas
Dr. Sas Conradie, DD, is the coordinator of the Global Generosity Network.
Though living in the UK, he was born in South Africa, where he is a
minister of the Pretoria-Oosterlig Dutch Reformed Church congregation
with mission calling.

EEN
The Evangelical Environmental Network is a ministry dedicated to the
care of God's creation. EEN seeks to equip, inspire, disciple, and mobi-
lize God's people in their effort to care for God's creation. This piece was
written as a collaborative effort by the board and staff.

Fouad, Maher
Maher Fouad is the general director at Arab World Evangelical Ministers'
Association. He was born and currently resides in Egypt.

García-Schmidt, Nydia
Nydia R. García-Schmidt, MA, is Americas Area Director for Wycliffe
Global Alliance. She has lived in the Philippines, Indonesia, and the
US. She currently lives in McAllen, Texas, USA. Nydia completed her
theological training in Mexico (her country of birth) and continued in
the US, graduating from Rio Grande Bible Seminary.

Gasser, Wilf
Wilf Gasser, Dr. med., is Associate Secretary General of the World
Evangelical Alliance in Berne, Switzerland. He was born in Switzerland.

Ge, Jun
Jun Ge, PhD, is CEO of Tree-Man Educational Consulting Inc., Beijing.
He lives in Beijing, China, and is affiliated with a number of organizations.

Gidoomal, Ram

Ram Gidoomal CBE, is chairman of the Lausanne Movement Board and Global Generosity Network. He lives in London, England, and is also chairman of South Asian Concern and an honorary member of the faculty of Divinity, Cambridge University.

Goh, Dr. Wei-Leong

Dr. Wei-Leong Goh, a family physician in Singapore, is the cofounder of HealthServe. He chairs the Christian Medical Dental Fellowship (Singapore) and is the Southeast Asia regional secretary of the International Christian Medical Dental Association. He serves with Operation Mobilisation and chairs the board of Mercy Teams International.

Heald, Frances Anne

Frances Heald, RN, is a nurse at Children's of Alabama Hospital in the cardiac intensive care unit. She lives in Birmingham, Alabama, and serves on the board of Friends of the Good Samaritan school in Mumbai, India.

Hillion, Daniel

Daniel Hillion is Church Relations Responsible for SEL France (a Protestant relief and development agency created by the French Evangelical Alliance). He studied philosophy (MA, 2001) and has published several articles on issues related to poverty, Christian social action, and Integral Mission. He lives in France.

Kuwana, Patrick

Patrick Kuwana is the founder of Crossover Transformation Group, where he serves as a Transformational Entrepreneur. He also serves as African Coordinator of Unashamedly Ethical and on the leadership team of Mission Africa Trust Fund. He is Zimbabwean and lives in Johannesburg, South Africa.

Lee, P. K. D.

P. K. D. Lee, I. Mech. E., MTh, worked with the Indian Government for twenty years and then with Haggai Institute for twenty years before retiring. He lives in Hyderabad, India, worshipping with the Centenary Methodist English Church. He teaches on Bible topics, leadership, and fund raising.

Madrid, Rony

Pastor Rony Madrid is the leading pastor of Iglesia Cristiana Vida Real (Royal Life Christian Church) in Guatemala City. This church is one of the largest churches in Guatemala.

Maramara, Zenet

Zenet Maramara, PhD, is the director of the Strategic Leader Development Center and director of the MBA in Biblical Stewardship and Christian Management at Asian Theological Seminary in Manila. She also serves as president of the Christian Stewardship Association and is the cofounder of Christians in Conservation in the Philippines.

Murdock, Pat

Pat Murdock lives in the US and is the former executive director of Issachar Initiative. He received his MBA from Regent University. In the past he served as managing director of development for the Billy Graham Evangelistic Association following a corporate career with Deluxe Corporation. He has been married to Holly for twenty-five years, and they are the proud parents of six wonderful children.

Offei Awuku, Christie-Joy and Eben-Joy

Christie-Joy (twelve years) and Eben-Joy (ten years) are siblings from the Offei Awuku family in Ghana, West Africa. They live with their parents and have a younger sister called Laura-Joy. Their dad is a missions leader with Scripture Union and the Lausanne Movement, and their mum, a medical doctor with a university hospital.

Patterson, Carlette

Carlette Patterson is the CEO of Patterson Sports Ventures and author of *I Thought We Had Forever*. She lives in Phoenix, Arizona, USA, and serves as the Sports Life Coach to Arizona State University Women's Basketball and Golf teams.

Power, Graham

Dr. Graham Power is the executive chairman of the Power Group of Companies. He lives in Cape Town, South Africa. Graham is the founder of the Global Day of Prayer and Unashamedly Ethical.

Ojo, Kehinde

Kehinde Ojo, BTh, is program director of Indigenous Support Development program of International Fellowship of Evangelical Students. He lives in Abuja, Nigeria.

O'Neill, Mike

Mike O'Neill is the CEO of Stewardship Services (UKET) Limited. He was born in the United States and resides in the United Kingdom. Mike is a trustee for Global Generosity Network, a member of the Evangelical Alliance UK Council, a member of the UK Advisory Board for Strategic Resource Group, and a warden for St. Sepulchres Church.

Ouedraogo, Philippe

Rev. Philippe Ouedraogo, PhD, is the executive director of AEAD (Association Evangelique d'Appui au Developpement), senior pastor of Boulmiougou Assemblies of God Church in Ouagadougou, vice president of AG Church in Burkina Faso, and president of the Alliance of Evangelical Schools and Universities of Burkina Faso (AESEB).

Queiroz, Edison

Edison Queiroz is senior pastor of the First Baptist Church in Santo Andre, Sao Paulo, Brazil, where he lives. He is the former executive director of

COMIBAM – Missionary Cooperation of Ibero-America, and the president and founder of ATG – Global Transformation Agency.

Rodin, R. Scott
R. Scott Rodin, PhD, is president of Rodin Consulting, Inc. and Kingdom Life Publishing. He lives in Spokane, Washington, USA, and serves on the boards of ChinaSource and the Evangelical Environmental Network.

Samuel, Richard
Richard Samuel is affiliated with Christian Business Men's Committee, Fishhook International, and Compass Finances. He was born in India, where he currently resides.

Trans World Radio
TWR speaks fluently in more than 230 languages and dialects. TWR exists to reach the world for Jesus Christ. Our global media outreach engages millions in 160 countries with biblical truth. www.twr.org

Tongoi, Dennis
The Reverend Dennis Obura Tongoi is the international director of CMS-Africa. He lives in Nairobi, Kenya, and is a DTh candidate in missiology at the University of South Africa on the topic "Business as mission and mission as business: case studies of financially sustainable Christian ventures in East Africa."

V., Chitra
Chitra V., in response to God's call, committed to serve Him as a full-time missionary in 2008 among the urban poor families in Bangalore, India, through Urban India Ministries and has served there ever since.

Williams, Gary
Gary Williams is the founder and national director of Christian Ministry

Advancement/Christian Management Australia. He lives on Tambourine Mountain, behind the Gold Coast, in Queensland, Australia.

Wills, David

David H. Wills is the president of the National Christian Foundation. He was born and currently resides in the United States. David is the chairman of the Global Generosity Foundation and sits on numerous other foundation boards.

Visit the *Christ Centered Generosity* website to read more generosity stories, share your own stories, dialogue with colleagues around the world, and find more resources to help you on your journey.

www.christcenteredgenerosity.com